CULTURE SHOCK!

Hong Kong

BETTY WEI • ELIZABETH LI

Graphic Arts Center Publishing Company
Portland, Oregon

Illustrations by TRIGG
Cover photographs from Horizon Photo Library
and The Image Bank

© 1995 Times Editions Pte Ltd
Reprinted 1995

This book is published by special
arrangement with Times Editions Pte Ltd
International Standard Book Number 1-55868-167-1
Library of Congress Catalog Number 94-076070
Graphic Arts Center Publishing Company
P.O. Box 10306 • Portland, Oregon 97210 • (503) 226-2402

Printed in Singapore

This book is dedicated —

by Betty Peh-t'i Wei to her granddaughters
"With love for Katharine Marie Garvin, Kiera Elizabeth
Garvin and Emily Margaret Garvin"

and

by Elizabeth Woo Li to the
feminine creative energy in her family
"Especially for her daughters Vanessa and Laura"

CONTENTS

ACKNOWLEDGEMENTS

We would like to thank the following friends and organizations for allowing us the use of their materials and publications: Heep Hong Society for Handicapped Children; Great Chefs; Hong Kong Land and Constance Ching; Government of Hong Kong (Government Information Service, the Department of Transportation and the Immigration Department); Hong Kong Housing Authority; Hong Kong Tourist Association; Institute of International Education and Marsha Lee; Provisional Airport Authority and Edith Cheng; St John's Cathedral Counselling Service and the Reverend Karol Misso; United States Consulate General, Hong Kong; the Academy of Performing Arts and Susanna Chan; and Kowloon Dairy and Eric Li. Frank Welsh's *A History of Hong Kong*, with its timely publication, has proved invaluable.

We are grateful to the following friends who have read individual chapters of the manuscript, and/or have contributed what they considered to be the ten most important issues now facing Hong Kong: Patricia Chen, Shirley Chen, Anna Chilvers, Frank Ching, Emily Colby, Susan Colby, Patrick Corcoran, M J Eu, Nelly Fung, Adrian Furnham, Geert Hofstede, Rosann Kao, Frances Katharine Liu, Richard Liu, Phyllis Lusher, Karol Misso, Suzy Moser, Hilary Prior, Jane Rice, Peter Riha, Priscilla Roberts, Elizabeth Sinn, Carl Smith, Beverly Sunn, Wendy Wong, Anna Wu; and others who do not want their names mentioned. All errors, of course, are ours.

The patience, courtesy, consideration, care and ingenuity of the editors of Times Editions are much appreciated.

Photo Credits

Builders Federal (Hong Kong) Limited 20, 27, 35, 46; Heep Hong Society for Handicapped Children 75; Hong Kong Land 9; Hong Kong Tourist Association, Singapore 8, 12, 15, 21, 48, 76, 81, 85, 87, 92, 94, 95, 97, 98, 102, 105, 118, 120, 121, 134, 144, 147, 157, 161, 165, 172, 174, 177, 178; Betty Wei Liu 58, 64, 72, 73, 91, 112, 164, 176; Provisional Airport Authority 127.

INTRODUCTION

Hong Kong is full of surprises, paradoxes and contradictions. Some are so obvious, so much a matter of routine or usually so well hidden that no one notices them.

The Bells of Nine Queen's Road, Central

Twelve one-metre high figurines of civilians and warriors in classical Chinese dress, each carrying a traditional Chinese Zodiac animal, ride on a carousel in a Western-style clock tower at Nine Queen's Road, above the bustling business district in Central. These figures, rotating on individual axles, come out of their nest several times a day to parade in formation forwards, backwards and outwards. They move their arms, nod their heads, and bow to the pedestrian and vehicular traffic, in time to the computer-operated music of twenty-five bells.

Whereas the appearance of the figurines is undoubtedly Chinese, the clock tower is derived from the Western tradition, as is the carillon of bronze bells with its span of two octaves. They were cast in the Netherlands, at the Royal Bellfoundry Petit en Fritsen, which has been producing bells since the middle of the seventeenth century. This quaint performance, so unexpected in end-of-twentieth-century Hong Kong, is all but drowned by city noises and is totally ignored by most passers-by. Nevertheless it is appreciated by discerning individuals who stop to look and listen. At least one pedestrian is tempted to risk her reputation for sanity, by returning the salute whenever she happens to be near when the bells chime.

The figurines and carillon in the clock tower illustrate how whimsically Hong Kong has adopted the traditions of China and the West. Not all aspects of this multi-cultural mix in Hong Kong blend so smoothly, however; nor is the blend always so palatable.

The carillon at Nine Queen's Road

The bells being installed by the maker's representative from Holland.

Ever-changing Hong Kong

Do not let street and shop signs in Roman letters delude you into believing that everything is 'just like home'. However well prepared you are on arrival, cultural misunderstandings lie in wait for you. As a new newcomer to the community, it is you who will have to adjust to the native culture, and the culture in Hong Kong is complex indeed. Be ready to see Hong Kong perpetually in motion. Appearances, as well as substance, can change every day. It is very important to keep an open mind and a cool head as you approach life in this city. Once acclimatized, you will enjoy the wonderful opportunities and life-styles Hong Kong has to offer.

This Book is Written for You

This book is written for you, an English-language reader newly arrived or expected in Hong Kong, to take up a job and make a home for yourself – and for your spouse, if you have one. It is also for short-term visitors who want a deeper understanding of what makes Hong Kong tick than can generally be gleaned from tourist literature. Besides giving factual information, an attempt is made to explain some of the prevailing attitudes and states of mind. It is our hope that, by gaining an appreciation of some of Hong Kong's complex and varied cultural traditions and institutions, you will reduce the frustrations of transition from your native culture to that of Hong Kong. Facts and background are not skimped, but our emphasis is on showing how you can adjust with greater ease; and, as a result, enjoy your Hong Kong experience more fully.

FIRST IMPRESSIONS

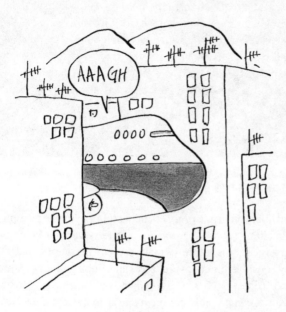

You can sense immediately the pulse of Hong Kong as your plane touches the Kaitak runway in populous Kowloon, on the edge of the blue waters of the South China Sea, amidst shrub covered mountains, and with a commanding view of the modern skyscrapers of urban Hong Kong. As the plane descends, you could almost feel that you are touching the multitude of television antennae on the apartment house roofs and reaching the laundry poles sprouting out of the windows. If you are seated by a window, you can take in the entire vista of Hong Kong in one full sweep as you land.

A panoramic view of Hong Kong Harbour. In 1952 Jardine House was the tallest building on the waterfront. Here, in 1993, it is entirely hidden.

Meanwhile, you hear a flight attendant telling you the passengers not to unbuckle your seat-belts and not to retrieve your belongings from the overhead bins before the plane comes to a complete halt. You personally consider this counsel utterly superfluous since no sane and mobile person like yourself, who commands sufficient verve to travel to Hong Kong, can possibly be so *gauche* as to contemplate starting his disembarking procedure before the plane has fully arrived. Yet, at the same time, you have become aware of an excitement generated by your fellow passengers as they take exactly the action the flight attendant was warning against, by piling themselves and their belongings into the aisles in order to push their way off the plane before anybody else.

THE NEED TO RUSH
When you are more accustomed to the local ways you will realize that this trying to get ahead of everybody else in every endeavour one

undertakes is a Hong Kong characteristic. It is not only that people feel it essential to arrive at their destinations in a hurry, they actually need to get there ahead of everybody else. This is called one-upmanship; Western terminology, perhaps, but a Hong Kong trait. At times, this quality is a positive and necessary one; it is what leads Hong Kong to try harder, in order to gain a competitive advantage over the rest of the world. It is only during the last ten years that ordinary people have had the opportunity to share in a prospering economy – where power and wealth had been held by a small privileged minority. This one-upmanship serves to describe the urgency felt by Hong Kong people, and in time perhaps you as well, in their race to achieve the often very demanding goals they wish to accomplish.

This urgency to rush out of the aircraft is a harbinger of things to come. What your antennae should be telling you is that, despite the Hong Kong Tourist Association's logo of a junk with open sails signalling a leisurely way of life, Hong Kong is not a sleepy fishing village of the Third World. You will live in Hong Kong under more pressure than at home if you hope to succeed here. Before you realize what is happening, whether or not you notice it yourself, you will be pushing and shoving too.

Since almost everybody you encounter personally in Hong Kong will be speaking English, or at least something that resembles English, and since the street and shop signs are bi-lingual – in Chinese script and Roman letters – it is difficult to imagine that anybody, especially you, would experience any cultural shock in Hong Kong. You see a fashionably clad and well-groomed populace, for instance, and instruments of instant communication: a fax machine in every home and office, a cellular telephone in every hand. Local English-language dailies are more than readable, and world-wide newspapers (*The Asian Wall Street Journal*, the *Financial Times* and *International Herald Tribune*) can be delivered to your desk before lunch. English-language broadcasts are available on radio and television. American-style fast food is on hand at strategic street corners;

bread, cold cuts and cheeses are found in delicatessens. Even bagels are freshly baked each day. So, how can you be wrong when you perceive Hong Kong as a Westernized modern community?

Below the veneer, however, there exists a society where traditional values and prejudices hold sway. Do not be misled by Hong Kong's superficial modernity; keep watch for deep-rooted traditions. No matter how seasoned you are as a traveller or as a resident in foreign lands, you will feel some degree of cultural shock. As a new arrival, you must be prepared – indeed, well prepared – to overcome this, if you are to make the most of the unique experience of living in Hong Kong.

A PLACE OF DIVERSITY, WHICH IS NOT CHINA

Unlike many Asian cities, where there is a native culture that can be defined because it is based on a single tradition, Hong Kong is a place of immense superficial diversity and contrast – and greater underlying complexity. Situated on the edge of a Communist monolith that is also the homeland of the ancient Chinese civilization, the polity of Hong Kong is a British creation. While the population is predominantly Chinese, the administration and laws are in the British tradition. It is a teeming city, with expensive boutiques vaunting the world's most celebrated names; yet the marketplace is still full of the cunning of the developing Third World. Hong Kong is an important centre of international commerce and finance, but the majority of Hong Kong's business undertakings are small and family owned. From the beginning, people of cultures other than Chinese and British have lived and worked in Hong Kong. Tradesmen from around the world have brought with them their own ways of conducting business and personal relationships, in accordance with their own cultures.

Circumstances of post-Second World War political and economic development in Asia facilitated the territory's growth into the modern metropolis of today; but old traditions, some long discarded in China and by Chinese communities elsewhere, still persist in Hong Kong.

An unchanging Hong Kong scene. Signs in English, Chinese and Korean show the territory's international character and reflect the congestion of the business district.

Eastern and Western cultures, not just Chinese and British, are found side by side. Without a command of Cantonese you will miss a lot of colour, but you still can get around Hong Kong.

Newly arrived, and overwhelmed by unfamiliar surroundings, you may not immediately appreciate the existence of the variety of cultures. Your senses are so bombarded, visually, aurally, and in every other respect, that it is difficult to react to the place with your intellect. You may choose to perceive Hong Kong as another Chinatown, very much like the one at home, only bigger and noisier – if you had such a neighbourhood at home. In which case, just as when touring your home Chinatown, you will note only the exotic features, or what you understand to be Chinese characteristics, without perceiving the Western modifications.

This deduction is difficult to fault, because ninety-seven per cent of the population of Hong Kong are ethnic Chinese, and are indeed

Chinese in appearance. In addition to over five and a half million ethnic Chinese residents and visitors, other Asians reside in or visit Hong Kong. Among the largest numbers of Asian residents are nationals of the Philippines, Malaysia, Japan, Thailand, Korea, Indonesia and Singapore. Many of these are of Chinese descent. To the non-Asian eye, Hong Kong looks Chinese. However, just as not all Asian tourists in Europe and America are Japanese, the Asians in Hong Kong are not all Chinese.

And you will not be the only one unable to tell the difference. A Cantonese banker of our acquaintance was walking down Chater Road in Central one bright Sunday morning, carrying in his right hand a heavy briefcase. He was wearing a pair of white trousers, an unfortunate choice as red hundred-dollar bills were rather prominently visible through his back pocket. This acquaintance also wears glasses and sports a crew cut. As he neared the corner across from what is now the Ritz Carlton Hotel, three youths accosted him. Our acquaintance felt a hand on his back while two men jostled him from right and left. Without thinking, and showing instant reflexes left over from his training as a private in the United States Army, he knocked down the man on his right with his briefcase, and held the man on his left in a half nelson. Meanwhile, as he spied the third youth with a fistful of his red bills, he swore at them in the exquisite street Cantonese he had picked up as a young student in Stanley. Taken aback, the youths returned his money and apologized: 'We are sorry. We did not mean to harm you. We thought that you were a Japanese.'

If you have never been to China, perhaps you will assume instantly that Hong Kong is another Chinese city. Under no circumstance should you commit the *faux pas* made by the Lebanese wife of an Omani businessman who proudly announced that they had been to China and visited four Chinese cities: Taipei, Singapore, Bangkok and Hong Kong. Please remember that Hong Kong is not China, and Hong Kong culture is distinct from that across the border. Even if you ignore the difference in clothing and grooming styles, Hong Kong people display a distinct countenance that bespeaks daring and self-assurance.

Or, if you do not look at the people at all, but notice only the Western-style architecture and the glamorous boutiques featuring European designers, you will get a completely different impression. Not too long ago, a Chinese American woman from Honolulu, who is married to a local Chinese, was asked by a tourist to point out the direction of Chinatown.

So there is a shot-silk effect. Depending on the orientation of your eye, Hong Kong is modern-Western but with underlying Chineseness, or it is Chinese with a surface of English-speaking internationalism. No one sees it as half and half.

BEAUTIFUL MOUNTAINS AND WATER

Hong Kong is on the coast of the Asian mainland. The territory – comprising Hong Kong Island, Kowloon, New Kowloon, the New Territories, and 235 islands in the South China Sea – has a land area of 1,070 square kilometres, or 400 square miles. Geologically it is a part of one of the mountain chains of South China where it runs into the sea, with the peaks remaining above the water as islands. The topography is dominated by steep granitic and volcanic hills covered with shrubs and grass. A large number of the outlying islands have no fresh water and therefore are not inhabitable. In the populated areas, however, there are sheltered bays as well as fjord-like inlets. Most of the beaches are sandy.

Your first impression of Hong Kong can easily be one of a concentration of tall skyscrapers amidst beautiful mountains. Carl Crow, a traveller of an earlier era when visitors came to Hong Kong by sea, noted in his 1933 edition of the *Guide to China* that 'there are grander sights to be seen in the world, but few more picturesque and graceful than that of Hong Kong – [especially] the entrance to the harbour and the panoramic view from the mountain.' These same mountains and harbour greet today's visitors still, whether they arrive by sea or air. Although the tall buildings that came into being during the intervening years have dramatically changed the silhouette of Hong Kong, the excitement of the mountains and water has not abated. The vista is still magnificent, although huge land reclamation projects have created more real estate by cutting down the sides of mountains. Regardless of how you fare in Hong Kong, its mountains and waters will remain a thrilling image in your mind for the rest of your days.

A PLACE OF EXTREMES

As befits an arena of worldwide competition, certain extremes in the lifestyle are worth noting. Hong Kong boasts the world's highest *per capita* use of cellular phones and radio pagers. While these means of communication make it possible for individuals to keep in constant touch with their homes and offices, thus gaining an edge over those without, they are annoying to others around them. As a result, cellular telephones are banned from many places.

Hong Kong has taken pride in enjoying a high consumption of protein, including a great variety of shell-fish. The claimed link between the traditional South China diet of salt fish and nose cancer may have no more basis than the purported connection between nose cancer and the penchant of the Hong Kong population for picking their noses. However, with worsening water pollution, hepatitis has become increasingly common. Media attention has been focused on unhealthy minerals in local seafood. Another study established further ill consequences of the high protein diet. The cholesterol count of rich-blooded Hong Kong residents has surpassed the United States equivalent. Heart disease and obesity among the population are of increasing concern.

The old adage that you do not get fat by eating Chinese food is bunk, as you will find if you eat like a native. But still, life expectancy is eighty-one years for women and seventy-five years for men. There are over 30,000 restaurants, including one with floor space of 14,000 square metres that can accommodate 6,000 patrons at a time. The largest night club in the world is in Hong Kong. It is said that patrons are taken to their tables in a Rolls Royce.

Hong Kong has the distinction of being the home of the world's first billion US dollar edifice, the headquarters of the Hongkong and Shanghai Banking Corporation. The desire to drive the biggest and costliest car available means Hong Kong leads the world with the largest *per capita* ownership of Rolls Royces, as well as with the highest number of Mercedes Benz outside Germany. In fact, the world's longest public parade of Rolls Royce cars, 114 of them, took place in Hong Kong.

. The world's first Braille edition of a daily newspaper, *South China Morning Post*, was published in English in Hong Kong. Hong Kong is Asia's most popular travel destination. In the year 1993, 82.2 million travellers entered and left Hong Kong. The world's largest wall of glass is at the Hong Kong Convention and Exhibition Centre in Wanchai, built on reclaimed land. The world's largest dredging fleet is working in Hong Kong.

Rural Hong Kong

Much of Hong Kong is urban, yet in spite of extensive construction of multi-storeyed new towns in recent years, almost seventy per cent of the territory has remained rural. There are still traditional villages, un-frequented woods, and wildernesses with wild animals. Country parks occupy almost forty per cent of the total land area. But as there is little flat land for the fast growing population, rural Hong Kong is giving way to urbanization. The Hong Kong Government has constructed new towns – from villages and new land. At the beginning of the 1990s, the rural areas often displayed evidence of abandonment and neglect; but many of the village houses now show signs of wealth. Common sights in Kam Tin, a village of the Tang clan, are large television sets in air-conditioned rooms, and luxury motor cars parked outside.

Urban Splendour

The curtain-walled skyscrapers during the day and the glittering neon lights at night make Hong Kong one of the most striking cities on earth. The Central District of Hong Kong Island boasts some of the world's most magnificent buildings. An early twentieth century geodetic survey showed that Hong Kong and New York, alone among leading deep-water port cities, stood on rock foundations that could withstand buildings of any height. With property prices quoted by the square foot, it is understandable that Hong Kong has developed upwards. For almost twenty years, the tallest building in Hong Kong was the 52-storey Connaught Centre, completed in 1973 and renamed Jardine House in 1989. Today, it is dwarfed by the many tall buildings of Central, Western and Wanchai, all financed by private enterprise and many designed by architects of world renown. The tallest building in Asia, the Central Plaza in Wanchai, is a symbol of one-upmanship, for it was designed to be one storey higher than the Bank of China Tower in Central.

New Hong Kong headquarters of the Bank of China, designed by I M Pei.

ARCHITECTS AND ARCHITECTURE

Building design reflects the local competitive spirit of free enterprise. Financial and commercial establishments vie with each other in their choice of prestigious architects and modern materials, with no expense spared. The new Hong Kong office of the Bank of China, designed by the American architect I M Pei, scion of a noted banking family from Shanghai, dominates the ground from which the ascent begins from Central to St. John's Anglican Cathedral and goes on to Government House. The bank also kept the original building at the junction of Queen's Road and Des Voeux Road, an imposing edifice of pre-1949 vintage. The Hongkong and Shanghai Banking Corporation is a formidable power in Asian finance – an issuing agent for

Twin pillars of the colonial era as joint issuers of Hong Kong's currency, the Standard Chartered Bank and the Hongkong and Shanghai Banking Corporation.

Hong Kong's currency and the principal depository of the Royal Hong Kong Jockey Club's receipts. A neighbour of the Bank of China on Queen's Road, it is housed in a wondrous combination of modern architecture and civil engineering. The new structure was designed by Sir Norman Foster, a prestigious British architect. With a desire never to be outranked or out-addressed, the Hong Kong and Shanghai Bank has assumed the address One Queen's Road, Central.

As a result of energetic campaigns by concerned residents after the demolition of the charming Hong Kong Club in the early 1980s, several buildings of the era before World War II have been spared from the developer's hammer. The clock tower on the waterfront across from Central is the only remaining segment of the old terminus of the Canton and Kowloon Railway, but the domed Supreme Court building, now the home of the Legislative Council, is still standing. Above the hill from Queen's Road, the French Mission of red-brick, built during the nineteenth century, has been renovated for use. The Cathedral of St John remains a graceful white church with a blue ceiling.

LANGUAGES AND SIGNS

Hong Kong is a bi-lingual society. Although the local use of English is becoming noticeably less orthodox, the language is still understandable if you listen carefully with patience and imagination. All street names, at least, are clearly marked in English and Chinese. There are good maps and directories in both languages. The Cantonese transliterations of the English originals tend to exaggerate on the side of auspiciousness, but they are charming and sometimes even clever. English translations of Cantonese originals, on the other hand, almost always make you stop in your tracks. If you are bi-lingual but cannot speak the Cantonese dialect, you may run into trouble. For Hong Kong appears to discriminate against Chinese readers who speak only Mandarin or another dialect. Non-Chinese readers will not have this problem, because to them, Admiralty is Admiralty. There is no confusion. For Chinese readers, however, the name of the Admiralty MTR station becomes 'Jin Zhong', meaning 'Bell' (so named because within hearing distance of the British naval headquarters); but, when pronounced by the MTR in Cantonese, it sounds suspiciously like 'Gum Jones'. By sticking to English, a great deal of frustration can be avoided.

On the other hand, even when you stick to English, you may be confused if your language training followed the American idiom. You may already know that you stand in a *queue* instead of a *line* while waiting for a taxi, and take a *lift* instead of an *elevator* up to your office. The use of prepositions in British and American English differs; likewise the presence or absence of the article *the* before a noun. You do not go to the hospital, unless to visit someone firmly in a particular establishment; as a patient you will go to hospital – a change of status from not being in hospital, which is more significant than the change of address. You will also spell *neighbour* and *labour* with the *u*. Whether you realize or realise it, the *Oxford English Dictionary* spells realize with a *z* but the *South China Morning Post* still insists upon an *s*, as in *recognise* and *sympathise*. Fortunately for you if you come from North America, criminals are put in prison here; so you will not have to face the confusion between *gaol* and *jail*. At least everybody is a capitalist, and you can capitalize on your sojourn here by becoming an Asian specialist.

CROWDS

The crowds in Hong Kong are immediately noticeable. During lunch time from noon to around two-thirty on week days, there truly is no space for the faint-hearted or weak-limbed on the city's pavements (or sidewalks). Jay-walking is a game people play all over the world, but where else do pedestrians need to queue eight deep for traffic lights to change, in order to cross the street? It is still possible to walk across the street without loss of life or limb, since traffic in Hong Kong generally does obey regulations. However, prominent signs denoting traffic fatalities are strategically placed throughout the territory to warn drivers; while pedestrians still leave much to fate.

Getting into an elevator (or lift) in an office is a serious challenge. First of all, no matter what time you find yourself in front of this vehicle, there will be a crowd assembling. The button, of course, will have been pushed already. Still, everybody – perhaps not you, but everybody else – will be pushing the already lit button, not once, but tapping it several times, like a barometer whose reading refuses to come down. When the thing arrives, the people inside will be pushing their way out, and your companions will be pushing their way in. Do not be horrified at this display of bad manners: there is so little space in Hong Kong, and so many people, that, if you do not rush ahead and take up the space, you will lose it to somebody else. And since the concept of private space is alien to Hong Kong, no one minds being crowded. Just do not lose your cool when everyone in your elevator crowd pushes the button at least a dozen times.

MOVING OPULENCE

Traffic is indeed impressive – not only for its sheer volume. In contrast to many Asian cities, it does move smoothly – albeit erratically at times when Hong Kong drivers are behaving true to form, trying to get ahead of everybody else. The roads are filled with luxury automobiles, vital symbols of their owners' status. Makers of Rolls-Royce, Jaguar, Mercedes, BMW, Toyota Crown and Lexus are enchanted with their sales in Hong Kong. One car in six is a Mercedes Benz; and one in every sixty, a Jaguar.

When in September 1991 the Rolls-Royce Company chose Hong Kong as the site of the longest-ever parade of its products, it was no random decision. With the Peninsula Hotel alone operating a fleet of eight Roll Royces, the Mandarin Hotel four and the Regent Hotel two – but the Regent has a fleet of twenty-three Daimlers – and a certain private individual said to own more than ten 'Rollers', one per cent of the company's production resides in Hong Kong. Glimpses (or, rather, sounds) of other high-powered cars – Porsche, Ferrari and Maserati, for instance – are also a part of the daily Hong Kong experience. If Cadillacs and other luxurious products of Detroit do not seem so prevalent here, it is because Americans insist upon driving on the right side of the road whereas Hong Kong traffic keeps to the traditional British left. Altogether, there were almost half a million registered motor vehicles in the territory during the calendar year 1991.

SMELL

As soon as you get off the plane, your nose will tell you that you are in Hong Kong, though what you notice is far less pungent now that sewers have gone underground. Various parts of Hong Kong have special smells. In Western, for instance, the atmosphere is permeated with the smell of creatures that once lived in the sea. For those who occasionally venture into the abyss of this district, the odour may be exotic. To the residents it is, understandably, offensive. The Urban Council tried in 1981 to license the local industry of shark's fin processing, in order to establish a certain standard of hygiene. Less than a dozen establishments had come forward to be counted, by the deadline. Hong Kong residents put hygiene requirements and the smell well behind their fears that, with more stringent standards, the processors might have to raise the price of the delicacy. This is known as the Hong Kong value system.

Of course, throughout the territory one experiences all manner of exotic smells. During the rainy season, clothes Hong Kong people wear tend to smell like wet laundry. When people live in high rise estates without laundry dryers, their indoor-line-dried clothes give off a specific odour that is especially noticeable in closed spaces such as elevators. Hong Kong residents are not as obsessed with cosmetic deodorants as Americans; so, during the long, hot and humid summer, your nostrils will be working overtime without enjoyment.

NOISE

The predominant language in Hong Kong is Cantonese, a Chinese dialect known for its complicated tones and colourful expressions. To the uninitiated, the language seems loud and harsh, nasal and guttural, all at the same time. Cantonese women and children, influenced by television, whine at the top of their voices. Their menfolk do not take a back seat in this respect. They carry on conversations on public transport and in lifts, at the top of their lungs.

Traffic noises are deafening as well. Although Hong Kong drivers do not honk so incessantly as their counterparts across the border, our drivers play their car or mini van radios just as indiscreetly. When the air-conditioner is on, and the windows are shut, at least the noise is confined to the interior of the vehicles. When the weather is cooler, drivers leave their windows open, and create additional noise pollution. In any case, when you are in a taxi, the driver is never content with fewer than two noise emitters: his radio connecting him with his central dispatcher crackling away whether or not there is a message, and the car radio tuned to a talk-show rattling away in Cantonese – or making a variety of sounds known euphemistically as Cantopop.

If Chinese restaurants anywhere in the world ever considered sound proofing, this novel approach to gracious dining has not occurred to owners of restaurants in Hong Kong. Despite sometimes luxurious decor, the decibels in restaurants are extremely high. It is not only the conversation of the diners at the tops of their voices, but thunderous noises in the guise of Cantopop rock, and announcements over loudspeakers: together they are deafening.

It is tempting to conclude that the noise bombarding Hong Kong is what makes the people of Hong Kong so grouchy all the time. However, before you decide to become a house-bound recluse during your entire stay, you should note that noise is associated by the Cantonese with happiness and togetherness; and that, to the ordinary Chinese in Hong Kong, silence signifies solitude and loneliness.

CONCLUSION

If your first impressions warn you that Hong Kong is a harsh place, please appreciate that it is also an exciting place full of wonderful opportunities. The people are industrious and they approach each day with anticipation. Once they get to know you or know who you are, they are also friendly and helpful. A few grumble about their rewards, but most are willing to work hard to achieve their goals. You must overcome your initial hesitations, if you have any, and become a part of the vibrant Hong Kong scene as soon as you can.

Exchange Square houses the Stock Exchange, the Head Office of Hong Kong Land, the American Club and many offices, galleries and bookshops. This prime property consists of three towers. The ground floor is the bus station – over which the towers were built.

— Chapter Two —

HONG KONG – ITS PAST AND FUTURE

It is generally known that Hong Kong owes its founding in 1841 to British merchants who wanted to expand their trade in China. From the very beginning a free port – in the sense that there was neither limitation on the articles of trade nor discrimination against any trader because of his nationality – Hong Kong soon became an important entrepôt between South China and the rest of the world. After 150 years, it has evolved into a major centre of international finance and industry as well. In an address to a gathering of scholars in August 1993, the Chief Secretary of the Hong Kong Government averred that 'Hong Kong's business is business' – still. In this regard, he was reflecting the perspective of the Government as well as reiterating the prevailing ethos of the community. At the end of June 1997, this free-wheeling community will be handed over to the People's Republic of China. The Joint Declaration of 1984 between the governments of Britain and China, and the Basic Law promulgated by the Chinese, have promised that the current economic and social system of Hong Kong is to continue for another fifty years, under the policy of *One Country – Two Systems*. So, until the year 2047 at least, *laissez faire* capitalism as practised in Hong Kong, with all its economic, political and social implications, is expected to continue.

THE CANTON SYSTEM AND THE OPIUM WAR

The Opium War (1840–42) is so named because the immediate purpose of Britain in sending warships and troops against China was to further the opium trade. This war had a tremendous impact on China, opening it to Western influences as traditional Chinese institutions and values began to change after the war. To understand the commercial and materialist character of Hong Kong, it is helpful to be aware of the nature of foreign trade in China before 1842 and of the circumstances under which Hong Kong came into being.

From 1760 until the Opium War, all foreign trade in China, except Russian, was limited to the port of Canton. Known as the Canton System, this single-port policy confined foreign traders to their quarters on the waterfront of Canton. Their families and dependants had to remain in Portuguese Macau. At no time were the traders permitted direct access to Chinese retailers, since all buying and selling had to be conducted through merchants franchised by the Imperial Government to handle foreign trade. They were known as *hong* merchants, and their firms as *hongs*. Articles of trade were limited, with the Chinese importing almost nothing from Britain, so British traders had to pay for their purchases in China with specie. To offset this imbalance, the traders smuggled into China opium grown in India, a commodity that the Chinese paid for in cash.

As time passed, the illicit opium trade became the most controversial issue between the Chinese government and British traders at Canton. Import, growth, sale and use of opium had been forbidden by imperial decree; but the quantity imported increased, especially after 1826 when officials at Canton became a part of the smuggling network. Between 1828 and 1833, British traders took from China 29.6 million (Mexican) dollars in silver, and the Americans another 15.8 million. This outflow of specie turned the balance of trade against the Chinese, considerably alarming the court because the drain of silver led to stagnation in the Chinese economy. In addition, widespread opium addiction among the populace, especially the troops, had become a serious problem. Therefore, the Chinese government pulled out all stops in enforcing its anti-opium policy.

Since the end of the eighteenth century, the British had tried to persuade the Chinese government to relax all trade restrictions. The Chinese had seen no need to respond. As the monopoly of the East India Company ended in 1834, and as the Industrial Revolution demanded an always wider international market for British manufactured goods, individual British traders in India and China more than ever wanted to end the Canton System. They lobbied Parliament, and eventually succeeded in securing their government's support through the deployment of forces to China. It was these traders who eventually set the tone for Hong Kong.

When Commissioner Lin Zexu (1785–1850) destroyed 21,306 chests of opium confiscated from British traders in May 1839, an excuse was provided for Britain to send warships to China. The British victory was swift, and several agreements were made, culminating in the signing of the Treaty of Nanking in August 1842. The treaty opened five Chinese coastal ports to British trade, and ceded Hong Kong to Britain.

THE CHOICE OF HONG KONG

The British Government had wanted consular presence at the Chinese ports, but it had not been London's original intention to establish a

British colony in China. If the creation of a British administered community on Chinese territory had been contemplated at all by British officials on the scene during the war, their first choice would have been Chusan, an island at the mouth of the Yangzi which had been a bustling port in coastal and maritime trade. Lord Palmerston, British Foreign Secretary at that time, could not understand why the British Crown or Government needed the aggravation of 'a barren island with nary a house upon it'.

Traders in Canton, on the other hand, had come to appreciate the deep and sheltered harbour of Hong Kong as early as 1836, and had envisaged it as the site of a British colony. A correspondent had written in the 25 April issue of the *Canton Register* that 'if the British lion's paw (were) to be put down on any part of the south side of China, let it be Hong Kong', and 'let the lion declare Hong Kong to be under his guarantee, a free port, and in ten years it will be the most considerable mart east of the Cape'.

Captain Charles Elliot (1801–75), Superintendent of Trade in Canton since 1835 and later British Plenipotentiary to China, was the first official to recognize the strategic advantages of Hong Kong. Elliot was the son of a Governor of Madras and a cousin of Admiral George Elliot of Elgin Marbles fame. He noted that the geographical location alone would make Hong Kong an ideal site for entrepôt trade between China and Southeast Asia – and with the rest of the world. The climate was favourable; at least its hot and humid summer was no worse than that of Canton, reasoned Elliot. Fresh water was also plentiful. The island was relatively free of residents, which was also an advantage.

Despite London's disapproval, Elliot directed British warships to take possession of Hong Kong in January 1841. British and international traders followed. A land auction was held in June that year, and the creation of Hong Kong was on its way. Colonel Henry Pottinger (1789–1856), later Elliot's successor, who had spent one day in Hong Kong in August 1841 before sailing up the coast to carry the war to the Yangzi, also found Elliot's choice attractive. When Elliot was recalled by London for disregarding Palmerston's instructions 'as if they were waste paper', British possession of Hong Kong had already been assured. Pottinger returned in early 1842; declaring it a free port, he stayed on as the first Governor of Hong Kong.

Opium, and Additions of Territory

Despite the significant role played by opium traders in starting the war, there was no mention of opium in the Treaty of Nanking. The opium destroyed by Commissioner Lin had been collected by Elliot from individual traders, among whom were some of the most cel-ebrated names in Hong Kong. William Jardine yielded 7,000 chests personally and 2,000 from his firm, Jardine Matheson and Company. Dent and Company gave up the next largest number of chests, followed by the Parsee trading house Heerjeebhoy Rustomjee, and the American firm Russell and Company. These firms were among the first to set up operations in Hong Kong. Hence, shortly after the arrival of the British, Hong Kong became a centre of the opium trade. An early issue of the *Hong Kong Gazette,* showing the cargo and ballast of each vessel in port, recorded that one out of every four ships bringing goods to Hong Kong carried opium. The commodity was usually transferred to smaller receiving ships, however, rather than being stored on shore. At first the traders were tolerated as smugglers by the British administration, but they eventually gained respectabil-ity when their businesses became successful – and more so when they no longer handled opium.

These firms also provided trade-related services in shipping, insurance and banking: for themselves and sometimes for other firms as well. As the volume of trade grew, a need arose for a bank in Hong Kong to handle foreign exchange, remittances and trade financing. Attempts were made by several London banks to begin business in Hong Kong and China, but they were not successful because they did not have local interests as their topmost priority. The Hong Kong and

Shanghai Banking Corporation, established in 1864 in Hong Kong, with its Shanghai operation starting a year later, was to enjoy a virtual monopoly over the financing of foreign trade with China. It became the premier bank in Hong Kong. The Royal Hong Kong Jockey Club, the Hong Kong and Shanghai Bank, and the Hong Kong Government have remained the most powerful institutions in the colony.

Soon after 1843, British traders yearned to expand trade in China beyond the coastal ports, and the British government negotiated to have a resident minister in Peking, but the Chinese were not responsive. The same wishes were also harboured by the French. When Chinese authorities boarded the *Arrow,* a lorcha owned by a Hong Kong Chinese trader but flying the British ensign, in search of suspected pirates, the British had an excuse to start hostilities in China once more. This war was known in history as the Arrow War or the Second Opium War (1856–58). British and French troops landed in Tientsin and marched to Peking, destroying the imperial summer retreat at Yuanmingyuan and driving the court into exile. The Treaty of Tientsin of 1858 granted diplomatic representation in Peking to the British and legalized the opium trade. In addition, closer to Hong Kong, the peninsula of Kowloon and Stonecutters Island in the harbour were ceded to Britain. The border between British Hong Kong and China became known later as Boundary Street, in Kowloon.

Towards the end of the nineteenth century, while Japan gained strength as an international power, China was losing control over its own territory. Rivalry between the imperialists intensified. In 1895, under the terms of the particular treaty that ended the First Sino-Japanese War, Japan garnered concessions similar to those of other 'treaty' powers in China. Before long, China was to be divided into different spheres of influence by the powers. To protect Hong Kong against all other imperial aspirations, Britain leased from China in 1898 the rest of Kowloon and an area north of Kowloon all the way to the Sham Chun (Shenzhen) River for ninety-nine years. Included in the same agreement were 235 islands in the South China Sea between Hong Kong and the Chinese coast. It is the 99-year lease for this area, comprising New Kowloon, the New Territories and the outlying islands, that will come to its predetermined end on 30 June 1997.

HONG KONG IN THE NINETEENTH CENTURY

At first, Hong Kong was the name of the colony, and Victoria was the principal settlement in Hong Kong. Queen's Road, the colony's main thoroughfare, also named after Queen Victoria, was the shoreline above high watermark at that time. Trading houses were built along the shore in Wanchai with business premises on the front and residences to their rear. The Chinese village at Wongneichong had been a thriving settlement and remained so for some time; but the newer Chinese businesses and residences were away from the shore in their own bazaars separate from the international business community, such as Canton Bazaar near where Pacific Place is located today, and in stalls where Central Plaza is now. It was these bazaars that gave the Chinese *hongs* in Hong Kong their beginning.

Within a short time, the *taipans* (heads of the major companies) – or their wives – felt the need to separate themselves from the lower-echelon employees of their companies, according to Chan Wai Kwan in his *The Making of Hong Kong Society*. They were also looking for a cooler location where the houses might take better advantage of the sea breezes. Therefore, residences were built on the Peak, 565 metres or 1,823 feet above sea level. Carl Crow described these houses in 1933 as being 'in tiers … perched on narrow ledges quarried out of the sides of the hill and reached by precipitous flights of steps.' Despite fog, humidity, and an ascent so difficult that it was possible only on foot or in sedan chairs, the breezes on the mountainside had made Hong Kong summers at least less intolerable. The Chinese did not begin to live on the Peak until after World War II. The non-Chinese middle-class, for the lack of a better term to describe middle-management employees of the trading companies, many of

A house on the Peak, designed in the 1920s for gracious living. Saved from redevelopers by limited access inherited from sedan chair days.

them Portuguese or Eurasian, concentrated their residences in Wanchai. Marriages between European men and Chinese women (as distinct from co-habitation) were carefully registered in order to protect the legal rights of the children.

Life was gracious for the Peak dwellers because servants, both indoor and outdoor, were plentiful. At first, furniture, luggage, alcoholic beverages, tinned food and all other comestibles deemed to be necessary for Western-style survival in an alien land, were brought to Hong Kong by ship. Gradually they began to be made here. There was little social mixing between Government officials and the *taipans* then, or between the *taipans* and the rest of the foreign community, and certainly even less between the foreign community and the Chinese.

Government House, where it now stands, was first built in 1855. The early governors and officials, unwilling to be identified with the traders who were definitely not of the gentry background, did not invite the business community to dine. This was the Victorian era, when class distinction was at its height. The more relaxed social atmosphere at Canton had not been transported to the new British colony. Forty-three persons in Hong Kong were considered to be socially acceptable at Government House in the mid-nineteenth century, but at the races it was another matter.

Horse racing had been held in Macau annually in February even before the Opium War so, after moving to Hong Kong, the horsy set of the international – especially the British – community duly attended the annual race meeting in Macau in the week of 20th to 25th of February 1843.

However, the ill-timed announcement issued in January 1844 by Governor Pottinger, also serving as British Plenipotentiary in China, that the British Government considered the territory of Macau a part of the Chinese Empire, had so enraged Portuguese authorities that participation or even attendance by British nationals at the Macau Race meeting was impossible. As a result, the most suitable piece of flat land on Hong Kong Island was appropriated to serve as a race course. Since the area was filled with muddy rice-fields, and was a breeding ground for malaria-carrying mosquitoes, it was named Happy Valley to confer a more auspicious aura. The Chinese call this area, more fittingly, Pao Ma Di – literally *Ground for Running Horses*. Both names have survived.

The Hong Kong Jockey Club was organized that year. To put priorities in Hong Kong in proper perspective, you may wish to know that St John's Cathedral was constructed in 1849 and land was not granted to build schools until 1873, but the first official race meeting was held at Happy Valley in 1846. Although the Chinese immediately caught on to the joys of betting on racehorses, they did not become members of the Jockey Club until after a number of them had played a significant role in settling the General Strike in Hong Kong in 1925. As an expression of acknowledgement for saving Hong Kong, the Jockey Club began to admit Chinese members in 1926. The largest horse-owner in Hong Kong at that time was Eu Tong-sen, the noted herbal medicine man from Malaya who was a legend in Hong Kong as the builder and owner of several European-style castles; the herbal medicine shop he founded is still operating at the end of the twentieth century. His stable had twenty-three horses. Sir Paul Chater, chairman of the stewards for thirty-four years, could boast only eighteen horses in his heyday. The register of the Club, dating back to 1935, shows that the first Chinese steward of the Hong Kong Jockey Club, Chau Sik-nin, the original owner of Dairy Farm, was elected in November 1946.

The Chinese in Hong Kong in the Nineteenth Century

Ever since the beginning, there had been Chinese in Hong Kong. The Treaty of the Bogue, concluded in October 1843, one year after the Treaty of Nanking and two years after the British took possession of Hong Kong, gave Chinese nationals free access to the new colony. This complete freedom of movement for the Chinese lasted until World War II. For the imperial Qing government in the 1840s, however, the transfer of sovereignty of territory to the British was a greater obstacle than consigning a population of 3,650 residents scattered in twenty villages, and another 2,000 on fishing boats, to alien rule. After the formal cession of Hong Kong, Elliot announced that Chinese residents in Hong Kong were under British sovereignty, and were, consequently, British subjects. Except for the abolition of torture in criminal trials, the Chinese were to be governed in accordance with the 'laws, customs and usages of China'. This pronouncement had the effect of segregating the Chinese residents in Hong Kong from the rest of the population. In 1844, the Chinese Government formally acquiesced to British jurisdiction over the Chinese population in Hong Kong; and in time, all laws came to be applied equally to all residents.

Two Chinese community leaders, who had accrued a fortune by provisioning the British during the Opium War, secured land from the Government to construct the Man Mo Temple on high land above Central in 1847. The Temple Committee later assumed leadership in the Chinese community, until 1868 when the Tung Wah Hospital Committee was organized. This committee then became the forum for the business and community leaders of the Chinese population. The founding of the temple reflected the sense of community responsibility of early Chinese leaders in Hong Kong. It was a public spirited gesture, to provide religious facilities for the fast growing Chinese community which was then made up of settlers from Canton and its environs. The temple was a place of prayer, and a repository for coffins until the dead could be returned to their native districts. From the outset, the temple acquired property around it, and so in time became extremely wealthy.

Traditionally it was not the state, but the urban gentry and the clan elders in villages, who assumed leadership in settling disputes, succouring the poor, and shouldering the costs of religious festivals and theatrical performances. These responsibilities embraced religious patronage, which included temple construction. In 1851, shopkeepers of Sheungwan were allowed to participate in paying for successive renovations of the temple, and it was they who elected the members of the Man Mo Temple Committee. Later, the Temple

Committee gained wider support from the Chinese community, by then expanded to embrace speakers of other dialects. The Man Mo Temple Committee was a major benefactor of the Tung Wah Hospital and the orphanage Po Leung Kuk, major charitable institutions whose committee members were also leaders of the Hong Kong Chinese community from the 1870s onwards. In 1895, the community had grown to 237,670 in a population of 248,498.

Christian missionaries, active in Hong Kong immediately after the British troops took possession, organized schools for Chinese boys to learn the English language and to acquire general knowledge. The Morrison Education Society moved to Hong Kong in 1842. It had been founded in Canton in 1835 by British merchants in memory of Robert Morrison, the first Protestant missionary in China, who had also served the foreign business community in Canton in other ways. Men trained in this institution later won renown in business, several serving as compradores for major *hongs* here and in Shanghai. This type of education did not equip them with the essential background in Chinese classics for the civil service examinations, thus depriving them of the traditional path to success as officials and scholars. But it did give them an opportunity to be of service to the then advanced-thinking officials in their attempts to modernize China. Jung Wing (1828–1912), for instance: he was a student at the Morrison Academy and the first Chinese to graduate from an American university – Yale College, the class of 1854. He proposed several projects to Li Hongzhang (1823–1901) and Zeng Guofan (1811–71). These proposals included manufacture of steamships, modern weapons and cotton textiles in Shanghai.

Towards the end of the 1860s, the importance of the Chinese in Hong Kong was beginning to be recognized. In 1865, 121,497 out of the 125,504 residents of the colony were Chinese. In 1869, when the Duke of Edinburgh, the popular second son of Queen Victoria, visited Hong Kong, he spent one day attending receptions and performances organized by the Chinese residents. By the 1880s, the bulk of Hong

Kong's wealth was passing into Chinese hands. In 1888, among the eighteen corporate and personal ratepayers paying more than $1,000 annually, seventeen were Chinese, and only one (Jardine, Matheson and Company) was British in origin. The Chinese did not take part in law making until 1880, when election of members by functional constituencies was being discussed between the Governor and the Colonial Office; Ng Choy, the first Chinese barrister admitted to the Hong Kong bar in 1877, was later the first Chinese to be appointed to the Legislative Council.

HONG KONG BEFORE WORLD WAR II

As the twentieth century opened and progressed Hong Kong became a sanctuary for Chinese revolutionaries and political activists. Sun Yat-sen (1866–1925), a native of Heungshan just north of Macau, and leader of the revolution that ended the Qing dynasty in 1911, was educated in Hong Kong at the College of Medicine for the Chinese. Sun had used a cottage near Tuen Mun in the western New Territories as his base of operations. The Qing government objected to this use of Hong Kong so the colony denied him permission to remain. He moved his base to Japan, where there were a great many Chinese students.

During the 1910s the international movement to abolish opium focused a great deal of attention on Hong Kong. By 1914, however, major interest in Europe and Great Britain went elsewhere: World War I started in August. Frank Welsh notes in *A History of Hong Kong* that 'German nationals were interned and German businesses closed down, and Hong Kong's Britons volunteered in great numbers, but the prosperity of the colony waxed, in part due to that old stand-by, opium.' Whatever the cause, the business community continued to thrive. The Kowloon-Canton Railway, linking Hong Kong to the Chinese hinterland of Hankow, was begun during the tenure of Governor Sir Matthew Nathan in 1905.

After the founding of the Chinese Communist Party in 1921, the cadres organized labour unions in the major port cities of China, notably Canton and Shanghai; and also in Hong Kong. China was under the control of the warlords after the death of Yuan Shikai. Sun Yat-sen had established a government in Canton, where he was advised by an agent of the Comintern, the international Communist movement. After the 30 May 1925 'Shanghai Incident', when students and labourers were killed by Chinese and Sikh policemen under the command of two British officers, general strikes started in Canton and Shanghai, and spread to the colony of Hong Kong.

Labour unrest first took place in Hong Kong with the seamen's strike in 1921, and subsequently against foreign shippers at the dockyard where Taikooshing now stands. The general strike in 1925 was widespread and more serious. There was a boycott of all British imports, and a prohibition on all ships using Hong Kong as an entrepôt. Hong Kong's economy was devastated. It was the colony's Chinese leaders who ended this spate of labour unrest in Hong Kong, as the political coalition between Sun Yat-sen's heirs and the Chinese Communist Party ended. From that time forward, Chinese leaders were recognized as a formidable force in Hong Kong. As late as 1930, however, left-wing unionism was still present in Hong Kong. In that year, the Vietnamese revolutionary, Ho Chi Minh, was active in Hong Kong in the service of the Comintern; but, when the Nationalists under Chiang Kai-shek took control of China and worked with Shanghai's financiers and capitalists, Hong Kong was able to breathe a sigh of relief.

ADMINISTRATION OF COLONIAL HONG KONG

Following the administrative pattern for a British colony, the Government of Hong Kong from the outset has been headed by a Governor, first appointed by Queen Victoria by Letters Patent. Members of the Executive Council and the Legislative Council were senior civil servants and, until February 1993, the commander of the British Armed Forces in Hong Kong was an *ex officio* member of the

Executive Council. The first non-official members, Thomas Paul Chater, an independent broker, and James Jardine of Jardine, Matheson and Company, were appointed to the Executive Council in 1896. Subsequent non-official members included *taipans* of the leading British *hongs*.

Until 1984, higher level officials were all brought from Britain, while middle and lower level civil servants were hired locally. Many of the local civil servants were educated at the University of Hong Kong after it was established in 1911. With the signing of the Joint Declaration in 1984, however, a policy of *localization* began to prepare for the administration of Hong Kong after the departure of the British. The sole language of government and the courts was English until 1973, when Chinese also was made an official language. Local officials, who are fluent in English and Cantonese, as distinct from expatriate officials most of whom have no command of Cantonese, began to be appointed to top Government jobs. Still, while expatriates accounted for only 1.2 per cent of the civil service, they held 35.4 percent of directorate-level jobs. Local civil servants, no longer grumbling behind the scenes, organized into unions and became increasingly vociferous in making demands with full press and media coverage. What we have today in Hong Kong is a new phenomenon: local Chinese in various fields receiving what they consider to be their just rewards – which until a decade ago had been reserved to a privileged, mostly expatriate, minority.

Besides the Governor, the most powerful officials are the Chief Secretary and the Financial Secretary. The Chief Secretary is head of the civil service, and is also the Deputy Governor. In setting the budget, the Financial Secretary is responsible for the fiscal, economic and monetary policies of the government. Both these officials are members of the Legislative and Executive Councils.

WORLD WAR II AND HONG KONG

The Japanese invaded China in July 1937. By 1938, much of China was occupied by Japanese forces, including the province of Guangdong immediately north of Hong Kong. An influx of refugees escaping from Japanese occupied areas brought the population of Hong Kong to more than one and a half million in 1939. After the Japanese attacked Pearl Harbor in December 1941, Great Britain, as an ally of the United States, was officially at war with Japan. Japanese forces marched across the border from Guangdong, and on Christmas Day, despite valiant efforts by the Hong Kong Volunteers, Governor Sir Mark Young surrendered to the Japanese army in a candle-lit room at the Peninsula Hotel. Until August 1945, Hong Kong was under Japanese rule. Buildings and factories were stripped, and materials were sent to Japan. Even libraries were raided and some rare items were taken from the University of Hong Kong to the Toyo Bunko. These books were returned after the war. The Japanese attempted to assimilate Hong Kong into their Empire, and proceeded to change the names of streets and buildings. The Peninsula Hotel, for instance, was renamed *Toa* (Great Eastern). During the war jobs were few and the economy of Hong Kong came to a virtual halt. There was a tremendous shortage of food.

There were individual heroes, however. British and Allied civilians were interned in Stanley on Hong Kong Island; military personnel in Shamshuipo in Kowloon. Sir Lindsay Ride, an Australian professor of medicine and later Vice-Chancellor of the University of Hong Kong, organized an intelligence network – BAAG, British Army Aid Group – to sabotage the Japanese war effort. Sir Lindsay escaped from internment by simply walking out of the camp. He eventually found his way to Chongqing, China's wartime capital, and won the protection and support of Madame Chiang Kai-shek. Although he did not succeed in getting the American Air Force to fly him back to Kaitak, he was present in Hong Kong when the Japanese officially surrendered at Government House on 16 September 1945.

Dr S W Kung of San Francisco, a retired banker who is conducting research on the history of the Bank of China, tells an interesting story of the old Bank of China Building in Central. When the Japanese forces occupied Hong Kong, in order to keep the Bank of China open, the army deposited a large amount of Japanese Army script with the bank. After the Japanese surrender in August 1945, the script became worthless, but the Yokohoma Specie Bank honoured it at face value. Thus the Bank of China had sufficient funds to build an office in Hong Kong.

HONG KONG AFTER 1945

The return of Governor Sir Mark Young to Government House was followed by a period of uncertainty because Hong Kong was expected to be reclaimed by China. In 1943 the unequal treaties the powers had forced on the Qing empire were abrogated, since China had become an ally in the war against Axis aggression. The civil war between the Nationalists and the Communists, however, which began immediately after the cession of hostilities, left the Communists ruling China, but diplomatically isolated. As a result, British rule in Hong Kong was not disturbed. Also as a result of the civil war, many refugees fled to Hong Kong. In 1931 the Hong Kong population who were British subjects totalled 73,866, comprising 61,640 Chinese, 6,636 Europeans, 3,331 Indians, 1,089 Portuguese, 717 Eurasians and 453 others – less than a tenth of the total population at that time. After the Japanese surrender in 1945, the Hong Kong population numbered about six hundred thousand. By the spring of 1950 it had risen to 2,360,000.

The new immigrants were of a different calibre. They were refugees, not small traders who wanted to come to Hong Kong to make a fortune, nor peasant labourers from Guangdong crossing the border to earn a subsistence. Many of them, especially those from Shanghai and Ningbo, had been bankers, entrepreneurs, financiers or industrialists; more than a few had come with their capital largely intact. Those without capital understood the value of financing and, working with the banks (sometimes hat in hand), they provided leadership in developing industry – textiles, garments, shipping, and electronics – and the transformation of Hong Kong into an international arena of finance and industry. It was partly due to the efforts of these entrepreneurs, observed Welsh, that 'during the 1960s ... Hong Kong acquired what have become its typical modern attitudes; that single-minded dedication to money-making which powered the engine of expansion ...'

The professionals – lawyers and physicians – especially those without English, could not transfer their skills into the Hong Kong marketplace. On the other hand, Hong Kong gave able and forthright women from Shanghai an opportunity to come into their own. Dame Lydia Dunn, born in Shanghai, became a Director of Swire's – and an active politician who spearheaded the efforts of the Hong Kong Development Council and served as Senior Executive Councillor. Anson Chan, the first local Chief Secretary of Hong Kong, was born to a family from Shanghai.

Development of the Municipal Councils

To handle municipal services, the Urban Council was instituted for the urban areas and the Regional Council for the New Territories. The councils, through the Director of Urban Services and the Director of Regional Services, take care of street cleaning, garbage collection, environment control, maintenance of hygiene in restaurants, food markets and abattoirs; control of hawkers; and maintenance and management of recreational and sports facilities such as swimming pools, playgrounds, parks, tennis courts, museums, libraries and concert halls.

The Urban Council has forty members. Fifteen are elected from the districts; ten are representatives from the district boards; and fifteen are appointed by the Governor. There are thirty-six members of the Regional Council. Twelve are directly elected along geographical lines, nine are elected as representatives of the district boards, and twelve are appointed by the Governor. The three *ex-officio* members are the chairman and the two vice-chairmen of the Heung Yee Kuk, a powerful organization of village leaders.

The urban areas are more Western in character than those served by the Regional Council. For instance, mainstream artists, such as symphony orchestras, ensembles or soloists from the West, give concerts in the City Hall Concert Hall or the Cultural Centre Concert Hall, under the aegis of the Urban Council. An Eastern orchestra or a Chinese troupe, on the other hand, usually performs in the Shatin or the Tseun Wan Town Hall – concert halls under the management of the Regional Council.

The Hong Kong Convention Centre is built on reclaimed land. It has the world's largest glass curtain wall.

The District Boards

In 1967, the City District Office scheme was introduced; there is no direct relationship with the Legislative Council. Members of nineteen district boards were chosen in 1985, but only about half of the 426 representatives were elected by popular vote. The other half were either appointed or *ex officio* members. The district offices located throughout the territory serve as direct links between the government and individual residents.

Growth of the Legislative Council

The Legislative Council owes its origin to British colonial practice. The first non-official members were appointed to the Legislative Council in 1850. The Chamber of Commerce elected its first non-official member to the Legislative Council in 1884, thus starting the tradition of functional constituency representation in Hong Kong. Understandably, all legislation proposed by the Government was passed, with very little acrimonious debate, until 1991 – by which time the representation of functional constituencies was wider and more varied, and the council had acquired its first eighteen directly elected members.

During the nineteenth century, even after the addition of non-official members, the Council had remained largely friendly to government policies. One notable instance of dissent was the position taken by the unofficial members on the repeal of the Contagious Diseases Act, passed by Parliament in 1867 to stop the spread of syphilis. This law required compulsory registration and examination of prostitutes in the brothels, and was considered to be inconvenient in many quarters, to say the least. Gradual changes of various minds in London led to the 'un-registration' of the brothels, but the repeal of the law was hotly debated in Hong Kong's Legislative Council. In the end, the majority official members voted *en bloc* to have the law repealed.

The reforms introduced by Governor Bowen, bringing non-official members in through the functional constituencies of the Chamber of Commerce and the Justices of the Peace, remained largely unchanged until the 1980s when more functional constituencies, representing economic and social sectors, were added. Since 1991, the Legislative Council has had a membership of sixty. Only three *ex officio* members remain – the Chief Secretary, the Financial Secretary and the Attorney General. Eighteen of the members were appointed by the Governor;

twenty-one were elected by the functional constituencies, and eighteen directly by voters in geographical districts.

In theory, the Legislative Council has gained the power to enact laws, but its major function has remained to debate government policies and the budget in public. Political parties developed.

International Relations of Hong Kong

Hong Kong is not an independent state. Relations between Hong Kong and other nations are in British hands, which is why the Governor of Hong Kong is chosen by the British Prime Minister on the advice of the Secretary of State for Foreign and Commonwealth Affairs. And that is why negotiations with China are conducted by representatives of the Government of Britain, and not the Hong Kong Government which – with an eye to the future – Beijing keeps at a distance. The Political Adviser is a senior foreign service officer assigned to Hong Kong to work with the Governor on relations with China.

Hong Kong's Coat of Arms. This emblem flies alongside the British Union Jack on the colony's flag.

RETURN OF HONG KONG TO CHINESE RULE

After 30 June 1997, when the lease of the New Territories comes to an end, Hong Kong will be handed over to China.

The British Nationality Act passed by Parliament in 1981 gave the right of abode in Britain to the people of the Falkland Islands and the people of Gibraltar, but excluded the much more numerous people of Hong Kong, regardless of ethnicity. In September 1982, Prime Minister Margaret Thatcher, aglow from victory in the Falkland Islands, went to Beijing to discuss the future of Hong Kong. Conversations with Chinese counterparts were neither cordial nor friendly. Hong Kong went into a siege mode as supermarket shelves were emptied of rice, oil and toilet paper. Two years later, the Prime Minister again went to Beijing. This time, there were results, in the shape of the Sino-British Joint Declaration of 26th September 1984.

SINO-BRITISH JOINT DECLARATION

China declared that it would 'resume exercise of sovereignty', while Britain's English-language version said that Hong Kong will be 'restored to the People's Republic of China'. As midnight ends 30 June 1997, the British Dependent Territory of Hong Kong will become the Hong Kong Special Administrative Region of the People's Republic of China. There was a pledge that the capitalist economic and social systems, the Hong Kong laws, and the judicial and educational structures would all be preserved for not less than fifty years.

Annex I of the Joint Declaration provided that the HKSAR will have its own form of government – with all its institutions intact, including a Governor and a high degree of autonomy. The HKSAR will also keep the right to levy taxes, which will be retained in Hong Kong. It may determine its own financial and monetary policies, and issue its own convertible currency. The People's Liberation Army will be stationed in Hong Kong, but it will not interfere in the internal affairs of the HKSAR. All rights and freedoms guaranteed by current laws will be respected.

The Basic Làw and the Joint Liaison Group

The Joint Declaration stipulates that a basic law of the HKSAR would be proclaimed by the National People's Congress of the People's Republic of China. The Basic Law was thus promulgated in April 1990. Summarized bluntly, the Basic Law declared that all Hong Kong laws then in force would be maintained, except in cases where the laws contravene the Basic Law.

Meanwhile, the Joint Liaison Group – representatives of the Chinese and British governments – was to meet at scheduled times to discuss the transitional process. The group has met in Beijing, Hong Kong and London. Problems over the rate of democratization (and their interaction with funding the new airport) produced a sour stalemate.

Issues of Democratic Development

In July 1992, a recent cabinet minister arrived as Governor of Hong Kong: Christopher Francis Patten. The appointment of a politician, rather than a Hong Kong expert from the foreign service, told Beijing that there would be changes in the five years before the hand-over. Governor Patten soon announced his proposed political reforms, notably the enlargement of the franchise for the Legislative Council elections due in 1995. The voting age would be lowered to eighteen, and the number of functional-constituency seats would not only go up from 21 to 30 out of 60, but would be chosen by an electorate expanded from a hundred thousand to nearly three million. This proposal falls far short of electing all members by 'one man, one vote'. Even so Beijing's reactions have, understandably, been negative. With deadlock in the Joint Liaison Group, Governor Patten may follow Hong Kong's constitutional procedure by referring his proposals to the (unreformed) Legislative Council; while Beijing growls.

George Hicks, in an *International Herald Tribune* article in November 1993, suggested that both sides were happy to have this opportunity to use the subject of democratic reforms in Hong Kong for political posturing. Britain was telling the world that before sending six million people to live under Communism, it was making sure that these people would gain a semblance of self-government. China, on the other hand, was showing its own people that Party cadres and Government officials were already controlling Hong Kong's future.

The Issue of the Through Train

'Through train' was a happily agreed metaphor. The Legislative Council that emerged from the 1995 election would continue its journey through 'Sovereignty Junction' in 1997, and beyond. There is immense symbolic and practical reassurance in this legislative continuity.

London, however, is driving a second through train – on a track leading out of colonial and into parliamentary rule. Mr Patten sensed that Hong Kong wanted faster progress. He was probably right in 1992; but, as 1997 approaches, fears of derailment increase.

To leave the metaphor altogether, Beijing's proposed counterstroke would not only preserve much of the 1995 Legco (as it will no doubt still be called) while ensuring its compliance; it would also influence electoral and other choices in Hong Kong for some time before 1997. Under this proposal, the members of the Legislative Council would be vetted in 1997 for political suitability. Members who were elected directly in 1991 are objecting to this imposition.

CONCLUSION

The economic importance of Hong Kong to China grows, despite political tension between governments. In 1988, twenty-nine per cent of Hong Kong's total external trade involved exports to and imports from China. Millions of Hong Kong residents visited China, contributing greatly to that country's revenue from tourism.

In June 1989 there were emotional and violent reactions in Hong Kong to Tiananmen Square. Nevertheless trade between Hong Kong and China continued to grow. In 1990, goods from China, valued at 236,134 million HK dollars, represented 36.8 per cent of Hong Kong's total imports. In 1991, the figures were 37.7 per cent/293,356 million; and in 1992, 37.1 per cent/354,378 million. In 1990, Hong Kong exported to China goods valued at 47,470 million HK dollars, or 21 per cent of the territory's total exports. In 1991, the value was 54,404 million dollars/23.5 per cent; in 1992, 61,959 million dollars/ 16.5 per cent. Re-exports were 110,908 million HK dollars or 26.8 per cent in 1990; 153,318 million dollars/28.7 percent in 1991; and 212,105 million/30.7 per cent in 1992.

On all counts, trade between China and Hong Hong has been consistently rising in value, and this upward trend is expected to continue. Where there has been a fall in mutual trade as a proportion of total trade, this should not cause alarm. It means that both parties are doing even better elsewhere. Considering the quantity and growth in Hong Kong investments in China, and of international investments in and trade with China through Hong Kong, it is not likely that China would disturb the status quo for the promised duration of fifty years.

Chapter Three

THE PEOPLE OF HONG KONG

Broadly one can say that, until the mid-1980s, there was a Chinese society in Hong Kong and an expatriate one – though this leaves out of account the Indian, Portuguese, Eurasian and Jewish communities. There were British *Taipans*, American businessmen, British civil servants, German manufacturers and Japanese *salarymen* – each more or less staying within their national/occupational group. Even among the Chinese, Cantonese kept to themselves, as did textile manufacturers from Shanghai, ship-owners from Ningpo and rice merchants from Chiuchow. There were people who crossed the lines easily and often, but such sophistication was practised only by a few. After all, conversations were conducted in the language or dialect of a group, so mingling was difficult.

As the twentieth century draws to a close, however, we see changes within and between the two basic societies. When multi-national institutions in Hong Kong no longer felt a need to employ Britons as managers, and when increasing numbers of ethnic Chinese – who had been educated overseas and were used to living abroad – returned to fill senior management positions, the lines that had divided the societies were no longer so clear. When English-speaking sons and daughters of the new breed of tycoons entered the family firm, the language of communication became English – and the style of conducting business less orthodox. Moreover, social life is no longer confined within ethnic groups: a cause and a consequence of the increase in intercultural marriages. But none of this means that traditional Chinese family-style business management is a thing of the past.

THE HONG KONG IDENTITY

How are the people of Hong Kong labelled? The terms Hong Kongers and Hong Kongese are beginning to be bandied about in the media; but somehow they sound contrived. Unlike the people of Germany who are referred to as Germans, of New York City as New Yorkers, of Glasgow as Glaswegians – and so forth – there is no single term in English that comes instantly to the tongue for the people of Hong Kong. In Chinese, they are known simply, and clearly, as *Hong Kong persons* – the name of the place followed by the word for *person*; but then, in Chinese, other peoples are called *Germany persons*, *United States persons, New York persons*, etc. This lack of a universally recognizable term for the people of Hong Kong is perhaps symbolic of the fact that no short label can adequately characterize them.

The Chinese population are beginning to assert their identity as Hong Kong Chinese, not least to stress their distinctiveness from the Chinese of China and the Chinese in Taiwan. Their insistence on continued use of *Can*tonese, instead of learning Pu*tong*hua – Manda-*rin* – (stressed so) in the schools was a source of controversy during the early 1980s, as was the issue of the simplified written characters developed in the People's Republic; but for various reasons there is no current public debate on these topics. Since 1984, with the pending departure of the British from top (and many other) Government jobs, and with increased opportunities in the private sector as well, Hong Kong Chinese have been demanding to gain control of their own affairs before July 1997. The rumour being circulated in Chinese cities as early as 1993 – that RMB (Renminbi), literally People's Currency, is legal tender in Hong Kong, four years before Hong Kong is handed over to China – only increases the determination of the Hong Kong Chinese to hold on to their own identity.

COMMERCIAL AND URBAN FROM THE START

From the outset, Hong Kong has been primarily a commercial and urban community. Not all the early inhabitants were British but, because the colony was, British firms were dominant. Even the first act marking British presence was a multi-racial one, reflecting the pluralist nature of the British Empire at that time, and subsequently of its colony Hong Kong. When Elliot took Possession Point in 1841, the troops he brought included 2,700 Indian soldiers. From then onwards, Hong Kong has welcomed people from all over the world – Americans, British, Chinese, Danes, French, Germans, Portuguese; Jews from Baghdad and Bombay; Hindus, Muslims, Parsees, Sikhs from India; and, in time, home-grown Eurasians. They were the traders and their employees, auctioneers, bankers, chandlers, charlatans, civil servants, coolies, lawyers, missionaries, painters, policemen, prostitutes, seamen, ship-builders, shop-keepers, saloon keepers, soldiers – and the newspaper editors who gathered and provided information. Perhaps not the Europeans, but some of their descendants have continued to live here, and have learned to use English and Cantonese, without being wholly absorbed into the Hong Kong populace. They have had to adjust to the prevailing culture but have kept certain traditions of their own; hence we find a multi-racial and multi-cultural society in Hong Kong, even without the expatriate residents.

The Non-Chinese Population of Hong Kong

The Portuguese had been trading with China by water since the days of Vasco da Gama (1517). They had established a foothold in Macau, but moved to Hong Kong in 1849 following the murder of Governor J M F Amaral. Except for the Portuguese from Macau, the European population in early Hong Kong was not large, and in this context the American traders were included among the Europeans. In 1845, only 634 of the Hong Kong population of 24,157 were European. They did not stay long because they came to make as much money as quickly as possible and return to their home countries. They suffered so badly from the ills of the sub-tropics – malaria, cholera, smallpox, dysentery, and the plague – that as early as 1844 British authorities actually considered abandoning Hong Kong. It had become known as the 'white men's graveyard', for many Europeans did not survive their tour of duty here. The Colonial Cemetery in Happy Valley, established in 1845, allotted separate sections for the civilian and military dead. Within a twenty-one month period, 257 men (the equivalent of an entire regiment) succumbed. The commander, General D'Aguilar, predicted the possible loss of a regiment every three years from endemic diseases. Shann Davies, in *Hong Kong Cemetery: Foreign Field, Foreign Devils*, counted graves of the Ninety-fifth regiment in the Colonial Cemetery: nine sergeants, eight corporals, four drummers, sixty-seven privates, four women and four children died in 1849.

Jews and Parsees in Hong Kong

Asian merchants who were among the earliest settlers in Hong Kong included Sephardic Jews from Baghdad and Parsees from India. The Sephardic traders in Canton and Hong Kong came during the nineteenth century from the Middle East by way of India, under the aegis of the Sassoons. The Parsees, Zoroastrians originally from Persia but settled in Bombay, were a part of the network of opium trade from India to China. Descendants of the first foreign traders in the metropolis became a part of the expanding international mercantile interests of that time. Their names included Belilios, Kadoorie, Moses and Gubbay; or Ruttonjee, Mody, and Rustomjee; some of which are prominent in Hong Kong today. They enjoyed business and personal links with the close-knit Jewish and Parsee communities in Shanghai and Bombay. At first they traded in raw cotton and general goods, and then took over the opium trade. Eventually, in Hong Kong as well as Shanghai and Bombay, they branched out into real estate, banking, shipping, warehousing, insurance, hotels, utilities and other industries, gaining power and influence locally as well as in the arena of international commerce. The first person from Hong Kong to sit in the House of Lords in Westminster was Lord Kadoorie (Lawrence Kadoorie), a member of the Jewish community in Shanghai and Hong Kong.

Indians and Muslims

From the beginning, the Indian community has been a major force in Hong Kong. Trade between India and China by land was of ancient origin. It was by these trade routes that Buddhism, Buddhist iconography and Buddhist institutions came to China. In modern times, trade surged during the 1920s, when Indian merchants formed an integral part of the network smuggling opium to Canton. These Indian traders, mostly Bohras from Bombay, first worked with private traders of the East India Company, and then set up business in Hong Kong for themselves. From handling opium and cotton, they expanded to general goods, and were joined by other Hindu and Muslim traders. For many of their descendants, loss of Indian or Pakistani nationality is not critical as long as Hong Kong remains a British colony. This group is now seriously worried about its members' status after 1997.

Except for Sikhs who came as a part of the military or police force, the Indian community is primarily a society of traders. The Sikhs, who have arrived throughout Hong Kong's 150 years, form the largest segment of the local Indian community. The first Sikhs came with the

A Hong Kong Indian celebrating Christmas.

British forces; later they came to work for the Hong Kong police. Some married Chinese women, and their descendants have merged into the Hong Kong populace and are indistinguishable except for their surnames. Perhaps because the first Sikhs had worked in law enforcement, it is understood that they cannot be enticed by Hong Kong's organized crime syndicates to rob their employers. Or perhaps it is because the Sikhs are thought of as tall and strong: they are often hired to work as guards for jewellery shops and other establishments handling cash. Resplendent in turbans that match their colourful uniforms, Sikhs stand out as doormen at leading hotels.

The Hindu Temple at Happy Valley has 12,000 members. Marriages are still arranged by parents, and are lavishly conducted. Once in a while Indians break into newspaper headlines, but most of the time they quietly follow their trades.

There are 50,000 Muslims in Hong Kong. Half are Chinese, or believers from Southeast Asian countries or the Middle East. Others came, usually generations ago, from India, Pakistan, East Africa and West Asia. There are four mosques and two Muslim cemeteries in Hong Kong.

Business firms of South Asian origin are strongly represented in the Hong Kong General Chamber of Commerce.

The International Community

The international community consists of more than Eurasian families, although such families have been an important part of Hong Kong almost from the start. Among the colony's wealthiest have been the compradores of the major *hongs*, one of whom, Sir Robert Hotung, was an early prominent Eurasian. Other families, not all as affluent, are still active.

Socially, the Chinese community remained separate throughout the nineteenth century. It had been an acceptable practice for certain non-Chinese residents to have Chinese mistresses as long as men did not flaunt their women before other people's wives. Difficulties arose, however, when the men were legally married to Chinese wives. One such problem arose when Daniel Caldwell, the Registrar General, married a Chinese woman.

In recent years, sons and daughters of Hong Kong Chinese families have gone abroad and brought back their foreign wives or husbands, creating a new Eurasian community. There are other American-Asian or European-Asian families. Depending on the native language of the mothers and where their children were born and reared, many of these children speak two languages.

A Eurasian marriage has a better chance of survival when living in the culture of the wife, or in a neutral culture. In Hong Kong, there are some wonderfully successful marriages, where both partners are mature and accommodating. We know of one English wife who lived with two non-English speaking mothers-in-law and a father-in-law. She learned to speak Cantonese, and brought up her children to be competent in both languages. It is to her great credit that she has adapted totally to the Cantonese culture of Hong Kong, while maintaining her sanity and independence and earning the respect and affection of her in-laws. Other Eurasian marriages make other compromises. One French wife shares her husband on Sundays with his mother. He goes to church and eats lunch with the wife and children, and takes his mother to the cinema in the afternoon by himself, making no demand that his wife accompany them. As long as the Chinese mother-in-law is not overbearing, and as long as the foreign daughter-in-law observes a certain amount of understanding and civility, cordial relationships can be maintained.

In fact, the Hong Kong culture should be an excellent place for Eurasian marriages and their children, especially if one of the partners is Cantonese. It provides opportunities to live in the cultures of both parents, and the children can acquire both languages. Except where a current wife is much younger than the husband or than a divorced wife who is still living, problems that may arise will be due not to the nature of Hong Kong but to universal difficulties such as money, or children from previous marriages.

The Hong Kong Chinese

Understandably, the dominant culture of Hong Kong is Chinese. Sixty per cent of the population were born here, but thirty-four per cent were born in China. Since the early immigrants had come from the province of Guangdong, bringing with them their dialect and their traditions, Hong Kong is predominantly Cantonese in character. Cantonese is the dialect spoken in the city of Canton (Guangzhou) and its environs. Dialects spoken elsewhere in Guangdong, Hakka or Chiuchow for instance, are not comprehensible to Cantonese speakers. (The characters of the written language are the same, regardless of dialect, but vocabulary and syntax can be different.) Hong Kong's popular culture is Cantonese, as is its street language (though with many modifications and additions to the original Cantonese tongue) so that the dialect spoken in Hong Kong has a character of its own.

Although English is the working language of the international business world here, among the older generation of Hong Kong Chinese, business and social conversations are still conducted in Chinese. While Cantonese and English are the languages of the Government and the courts, Putonghua is used with increasing frequency. Minority ethnic groups, such as established Hindus or Sikhs, retain their ancestral languages at religious ceremonies, but they read and write English and also speak Cantonese. As a generalization, it is safe to say that the population of Hong Kong speaks and thinks in Cantonese.

Have the Hong Kong Chinese become more westernized than their counterparts in China and Taiwan? If so, is it because they have been living under British influence for over 150 years? The daily lives of Hong Kong Chinese have long been made comfortable by Western/Japanese gadgetry not enjoyed by their counterparts in Taiwan and the mainland until recently. Besides television and karaoke, the people are blessed with indoor plumbing and contact lenses. In many respects, British Hong Kong has surpassed even the most advanced western countries in modernity, while retaining traditions abandoned on the mainland as China underwent successive political and modernization programmes during the past fourscore years. In superficial appearance and social attitude, the Hong Kong Chinese may have changed beyond recognition since the days immediately after the Opium War; but, as they were indoctrinated by Confucius and their parents long before making the acquaintance of Adam Smith or Georgio Armani, their thinking has remained essentially Chinese.

HOW DO THE CHINESE SEE THEMSELVES?

Ethnic Chinese, whether in China, Hong Kong or overseas, seldom think of fellow Chinese in terms of being just Chinese: Cantonese, Sichuanese, Shanghainese, yes, but never Chinese as a category. Strictly speaking, not everyone whose forebears had come from various counties of the Guangdong Province – Taishan or Chiuchow, for example – should be lumped together into a single category as

Cantonese; but when we speak in English the word Cantonese usually denotes people from the Guangdong province as a whole. The Cantonese-speaking public of Hong Kong, meanwhile, tends to describe all who do not command perfect Cantonese as Shanghainese or, on rare occasions, Shangdongese. However this practice is diminishing as more Chinese who speak northern dialects move into Hong Kong, and as local Cantonese-speakers begin to distinguish one non-Cantonese dialect from another.

Some non-Chinese who have lived in Hong Kong for a long time also catch on to this way of thinking. A Cantonese-speaking senior government official from Britain informed the woman seated to his right at a dinner party some time during the early 1980s that he was puzzled in trying to categorize her. She was 'not a Hong Kong Chinese, not of the Shanghai textiles group, nor a Taiwanese intellectual'. While the woman would much rather have been acknowledged as a unique Chinese individual in Hong Kong who did not play mahjong, she appreciated the fact that he had managed to synthesise the Chinese propensity to categorize people geographically with the Hong Kong tendency to put people in their socio-economic groupings. Being an individual standing or falling on one's own merits is too alien a concept for nearly all Chinese, a concept this Briton had absorbed through his long association with the locals.

The Masses of Hong Kong

Although a handful of Hong Kong names are listed among the world's wealthiest in *Fortune* and *Forbes*, more than half of the masses live in public housing estates. They work hard and live frugally; they are not a part of the luxurious lifestyle of Hong Kong. The over-all population density was 5,700 per square kilometre in 1993, ranging between 26,180 per square kilometre in the metropolitan area and 2,790 per kilometre in the rural area. In 1992 these last two figures were, respectively, 26,450 and 2,700 – showing a shift in the population's centre of gravity towards new towns in the New Territories.

The Economist gives Hong Kong's *per capita* income in 1990 as US$10,500. Compared to India's US$270, Portugal's US$5,200, Ireland's US$9,624 – and even Singapore's US$10,800, and US$15,300 for the United Kingdom – it is impressive. Government statistics for 1992 show that seventy-five per cent of the industrial workers received US$22 a day or more, revealing that twenty-five per cent of the workers received less. Government statistics also show that wage increases had lagged behind the rate of inflation. To cover expenses, more than one member of a family needs to earn, usually the father, and daughters when they reach the age of fifteen. Certain fathers work at two jobs, and for many of these the second is driving the evening-night shift of taxicabs. Men receive higher wages than women, but families still educate sons beyond the school leaving age of fifteen and put their daughters to work. As an expatriate, you will encounter the Hong Kong masses daily even if you do not live in a public housing estate or travel by public transport. The masses deliver your newspapers and letters, cut your hair, sell you fruits and flowers, ride the lifts in your building, and work in your office.

The 'Middle Class'

Until the 1980s, it could be said truly that the people of Hong Kong were divided into those who had and those who had not, with all the economic and social implications of those terms. Then public and private sectors began to hire local Chinese for professional and management jobs. For the first time, locally hired employees in private companies, and civil servants – as distinct from those re-cruited overseas – are able to rise beyond middle echelon jobs. An increasing number of local Chinese enjoy sufficient income to buy their own homes, send their children to fee-charging schools, run cars, and take holidays abroad. Second salaries enable families to enjoy the services of imported domestics, and the domestics allow mothers to earn the extra salary outside the home to free themselves from the drudgery of house-keeping. It is this group – hard pressed, but more

The fruit vendor of Macdonnell Road: a human-scale market in a residential street.

'have' than 'have not' – that demands greater political participation in public affairs. It is also this group that voices its insistence on a continuing Hong Kong identity.

THE TRIADS

Anti-establishment secret brotherhoods, popularized in picaresque novels, the best known of which is the *Shuihuzuan* – translated into English as *All Men Are Brothers* or *Water Margin* – have been a part of life in the lower strata of Chinese society for more than a thousand years. During the middle of the nineteenth century, when economic and social conditions made rebellion against the alien Qing rulers inevitable, many of these societies were revived as seditious as well as criminal gangs. Despite official efforts at suppression, the societies grew. Among the longest-surviving of the societies in South China was the Three Dots Society, known here to contemporary Westerners as the Triad, or overseas as the Chinatown gang, the *tong*.

No longer political, modern Triads in Hong Kong are involved in all aspects of crime. It is understood that the Hong Kong Triads have taken over the drug trade from the Mafia in Europe and America. In Hong Kong, they control rings of extortion, drug manufacture and distribution, pornography, counterfeiting, robbery and vice. Bank and jewellery shop robbers in Hong Kong used to wield the chopping knife. Today, Triad members are smuggled in from Guangdong and threaten their victims with handguns and grenades. Law enforcement officials are concerned with the spread of Triads in schools, but the chances of you, as an expatriate, having any direct encounter with the them are minute. The Triads will continue to plague Hong Kong, regardless of the 1997 watershed.

IMPORTANCE OF EDUCATION

Traditionally, in theory at least, China was a meritocracy, run by an officialdom of men who had passed the required series of civil service examinations – irrespective of their family background. To succeed in these examinations, a thorough grounding in the Classics was essential; hence the emphasis on education almost since time immemorial. Although Hong Kong's traditions are material rather than intellectual, Hong Kong businessmen have always sent their children to the most prestigious schools and universities they could afford. Until recently, when other considerations began to intervene, family ambitions were for able sons and daughters to attend the University of Hong Kong in their undergraduate years, to build up a network of acquaintances useful in later life.

Gradually, they were sent to universities in the United Kingdom instead. Then, as Hong Kong became more international, students headed for colleges and universities in Australia, Canada and the United States. There is no indication whether this trend relates to aspirations for future residence. American degrees are increasingly popular with Hong Kong employers, especially when granted by institutions with snob appeal. Records kept by the Institute of International Education in New York City show that during the early 1960s, fewer than 800 students from Hong Kong were studying in American colleges and universities; in the 1964–65 academic year, 3,279 Hong Kong students were registered. The numbers increased steadily until there were 11,230 in the academic year of 1989–90, 12,603 in 1990–91 and 13,190 in 1991–92 The American Consulate General in Hong Kong issued an average of 451 visas each month to Hong Kong students to study in the United States in 1992, and the monthly average for 1993 was 474. These numbers do not include students who enter the United States on immigrant visas.

Although Hong Kong now has three universities and five other tertiary level institutions which grant degrees and diplomas, several factors will probably maintain the upward trend in foreign university study. First, the old instinct for higher education is coupled with the new competitive paper chase. Second, the expanding middle class includes graduate parents of school leavers. Third, Hong Kong may become a channel to Western universities for its non-HKSAR Chinese residents.

EMIGRATION

Although the people of Hong Kong have been British subjects for more than 150 years, and many of them carry British passports, they do not consider themselves British. They owe allegiance to the Queen but, with few exceptions, do not enjoy full civil and political rights as citizens of the United Kingdom of Great Britain and Northern Ireland. Only a limited number of people from Hong Kong with certain specific qualifications may apply for the right of abode in the British Isles. Hong Kong people hold different types of travel document, including the British National (Overseas) passport and something called the Hong Kong Certificate of Identity. Even before 1997, neither enjoys the same status internationally as a British passport issued in London. Their value after June 1997 is a matter of serious concern.

Despite China's avowal that Hong Kong's economic system and institutions will be preserved for fifty years after 30 June 1997, not all the Hong Kong people are convinced. Those of non-Chinese ethnic origin are concerned, because they are not persuaded that the Chinese Government will respect their rights in Hong Kong. The Hong Kong Chinese worry even more. In addition to their distrust of London and Beijing, they are anxious about China's ability to manage Daya Bay, the nuclear plant just north of the border, in Guangdong. The masses have no choice, but those who could afford to establish residence qualifications elsewhere have been finding places that would welcome them.

During the early 1980s, people who could see the writing on the wall started to buy houses in Australia, the United States or Canada. California and Vancouver are popular because they are least distant from Hong Kong, and because their climates are mild. Sydney is the most desired of the Australian cities. Men leave their families in the new home to fulfil the residency requirements, while they themselves commute to Hong Kong to take care of their business. They are known as the 'Hong Kong Astronauts' because they spend so much time in the air. From 1982 to the mid-1980s, an average of 20,000 people left Hong Kong each year to settle abroad; they did not sever their ties with Hong Kong, and many have returned – with new nationalities and new passports.

After the signing of the Joint Declaration in 1984, annual departures rose to 30,000 in 1987 and to 66,000 in 1992. In 1993, because of decreasing employment opportunities in the destination countries, the number of emigrants was estimated to have fallen to 54,000. Hong Kong feels particularly keenly the absence of younger professionals who take their families overseas without intending to return. Of the 60,000 emigrants (including wives and children) who left in 1991, 21,000 had held administrative, managerial or technological positions in government or the private sector. Preferred destinations were the English-speaking Commonwealth countries of Canada and Australia. Few chose to go to Britain. With the quota constraints, there is a queue of 120,000 awaiting clearance into the United States. The older generation tends to opt for Singapore, because the lifestyle of that Southeast Asian country is more to their liking.

To offset the losses from its professional work force, the Hong Kong Government is working with the Chambers of Commerce on programmes to entice back people whose skills are needed. Depressed economic conditions in the host countries are leading more emigrants to return and take up employment in Hong Kong. Government statistics show that 43,000 (twelve per cent) of people who emigrated between 1982 and 1991 have returned to Hong Kong; 14,000 (nine per cent) of 1980-1989 emigrants have come back.

The Hong Kong Schools

There is compulsory education in Hong Kong until the age of fifteen. All Government primary schools up to the sixth grade teach in Cantonese, apart from English as a subject. The Anglo-Chinese schools give instruction in English at secondary level, with maybe Chinese and Chinese history taught in Cantonese, all the way through to 'A' Level examinations. The best known of the handful using Putonghua (Mandarin) instead of Cantonese are the Kiangsu-Chekiang schools. English-speaking children are educated from primary to 'A' Level at the English Schools Foundation schools, where the UK curriculum is followed. Each international school uses the curriculum of its country of origin – the French International School, the French schools curriculum, for instance; and the Hong Kong International School, the American curriculum. The French International School teaches in French and the German-Swiss International School teaches in German, although in each case there is also an English stream. Several international schools here follow the International Baccalaureate programme. Fees vary among private schools.

The return of earlier emigrants with their school-age children led to the growth of the international school system in Hong Kong. When children have been away for two or more years, it is difficult if not impossible for them to return to the local school system, especially since they will have studied no Chinese while abroad. The system cannot accommodate students who weave in and out at different stages. However, some parents are unwilling for their children to give up Chinese completely. As a result, new schools have emerged to serve families who want their children to learn both English and Chinese. The Canadian Chamber of Commerce opened the Canadian International School, which brought the teaching of Cantonese into the curriculum; and the Singapore Government opened the Singapore International School, offering the official curriculum of Singapore schools. This includes Mandarin as a subject, and culminates in Cambridge 'O' and 'A' Level examinations There is great demand for places at the Chinese International School, which in 1982 pioneered a curriculum in English and Mandarin; it requires students to study Chinese language, history and culture at all levels of the school. The Chinese International School and the French International School offer the International Baccalaureate Programme. The recently opened Li Po Chung College, a pre-university school of the United World

College system, also offers this programme. Half of its student body is local, the others coming from overseas.

Northern Cousins in Liberated Zones

So many people leaving Hong Kong does not mean more room for you on the streets. While Hong Kong's birthrate has declined since the 1960s, population has continued to rise through immigration. Immigrants arrive daily from China. (In 1993, 32,900 Chinese moved across the border legally as settlers, including 13,250 wives, 1,370 husbands and 14,504 children of – in all cases – legal Hong Kong residents. In 1992 the equivalent figures had been smaller; 28,400 including 11,128 wives, 1,082 husbands and 12,457 children.) Illegal immigrants are entering at an average rate of 130 daily, many working on construction sites. Road blocks are set up to inspect vehicles for such immigrants, and regular checks are made at construction sites to search them out. As soon as they are discovered, they are bound in rough ropes and repatriated to China, where – declared the Governor of Guangdong in May 1993 – they are incarcerated. But still they come, in droves, to work at construction sites for unscrupulous contractors with an eye for quick bucks.

Increasingly, citizens of the People's Republic of China are living and working legally in Hong Kong. Twenty per cent of shares traded on the Hong Kong Stock Exchange are those of companies owned by mainland Chinese interests. No longer the *nouveaux pauvres* of the world, Chinese businessmen populate some of Hong Kong's most prestigious clubs, wielding knives and forks as if to the manner born; which in a sense they must have been, in order to enjoy the privilege of being assigned to jobs in Hong Kong. However, this is perhaps not a fair assessment of the *Northern Cousins* in Hong Kong – as they are called somewhat condescendingly by the local Chinese, because of their lack of sophistication and their inability to communicate in Cantonese. They tend to congregate in certain areas, such as Wanchai, Western and North Point, where the rents are more affordable and where they have acquired property, causing the areas to be nicknamed the *Liberated Zones* of Hong Kong. However, in fast-moving Hong Kong, this generalization is ceasing to be true. PRC people are moving into prestigious neighbourhoods, outbidding local investors in buying flats, and driving property prices up.

We must correct this under-assessment in another context also. Many young men and women from China, educated overseas with professional degrees and a full command of English, are working in international companies in Hong Kong. The Associate Concert Master of the Hong Kong Philharmonic Orchestra, for example, was trained at the Juilliard School of Music. She hails from Shanghai.

Expatriates

The term 'expatriate', or 'expat' for short, defined in the Oxford English Dictionary as one who lives outside his own country by choice, may sound better than 'foreigner'. An expat is understood here as a resident of Hong Kong whose native culture is not that of a Hong Kong Chinese.

How will the locals view you? Regardless of your nationality, you will be a foreigner; but, if you are ethnic Chinese, you will also be a Chinese no matter how many generations of your ancestors have lived abroad. After all, China has been the centre of the world for a long, long time; so any non-Chinese in China is known as a *foreigner*, an *ocean person* (a person from across the ocean) or an *ocean ghost* (a ghost from across the ocean).

Thus, more informally, if you are Caucasian in appearance, you will be referred as a *gweilo* (a male devil or ghost) or as a *gweipo* (a female ghost) or *gweizai* (boy ghost) or *gweinui* (girl ghost) – depending on your gender and seniority. Similarly, if you are African in appearance, you will be a *hagwei* (black ghost), and so on. Do not be offended. These terms are not necessarily derogatory. It has become a custom to think of ethnic non-Chinese in our midst in such terms. As a matter of fact, they can even be considered friendly

71

An American family reunion on the Peak, with four generations plus dogs. Note the China Coast School oil painting that shows foreign hongs in Canton before the Opium War.

salutations, used to show a sense of familiarity – when the Chinese are usually far less personal. This does not mean that you need to express gratitude and pleasure for this dubious distinction, however. Increasingly, expats in Hong Kong resent being called *devils*. Perhaps they feel less secure than their predecessors.

As long as the local population does not live in close proximity with the expats, dealing with each other only in the office, so to speak, relationships will remain cordial. There is a language gap; so, when there are failures in communication, a feeling of resentment on both sides may be intensified. (If both sides think about it, though, they should realise that such failures are mainly linguistic but partly cultural; since they are not caused by hostility, they should not lead to hostility.) Alas few expatriates have managed to learn Cantonese, principally because the language is not easy to master but also because they would have no use for it elsewhere. When they complain about the English language capability of a local individual, their attitude can be interpreted as condescending; when this is so, it is resented by the local. In 1993 there was a spate of letters in *Letters to the Editor* columns from expatriate residents about behaviour by the local population. Some of the complaints show the local offenders to be rude; others are funny, but even the humour of the situation does not mitigate the embarrassment and hurt felt by the expat victims. So far, skirmishes have been minor. The local population, on the whole, has contained its resentment. As long as each side is willing to remain polite, clashes are avoidable – even in these peculiarly difficult circumstances, where *de facto* control is transferring itself ahead of the *de jure* calendar.

If your company will pay for you to live in one of these view-spoiling structures, you will yourselves enjoy superb views.

73

The Expat Spouse

In recent years, a spate of young and single expatriates has poured out of universities or business schools to seek employment in Hong Kong, because of the depressed economies of their home countries. Most expats, however, are experienced executives and professionals and many are sent by international companies. Few have left their families behind. There is intense pressure on them to produce profits, if for no other reason than to cover their salaries and overheads. The rule of thumb is: the higher the package, the harder the expatriate is expected to work. Often there is a great deal of regional travel. While it may be beneficial to accrue frequent-flyer mileage, the hectic schedule can be costly in physical and emotional terms. Bebe Chu, a solicitor practising family law, reveals that temptations here are tremendous. It takes a special man or woman, and a very strong marriage, to survive Hong Kong.

There are more expat wives than husbands of expats. The latter species is increasing though. For spouses of expatriate executives whose employment terms give them luxuries not always available at home, such as domestic servants, club membership, prestigious addresses, private schools, annual paid home leave – which translates into international travel, or even spendable cash – life should be comfortable indeed. Most expatriate spouses adjust well to Hong Kong, many in inimitable style, and are taking advantage of life in Asia. Many women acquire skills they have always wanted. One woman we know gained a doctorate from the University of Hong Kong. Others are working on master's degrees or learning Chinese. One father takes his infant daughter to the office three days a week, while his wife works – actively shouldering fifty per cent of the child-care and household responsibilities. Perhaps under similar circumstances this man would do as much had he stayed in his own culture, but unfortunately not all foreign families overcome their culture shock so satisfactorily.

Newly arrived wives tend to stick together with other expatriate wives, if indeed they manage to meet each other. Those with children find it easier because they see mothers of their children's school-mates. It is difficult to make friends with the local Chinese, as a rule, even when the expat wife is of Chinese origin. It is also difficult for returned Chinese to pick up relationships they had before they left. Or they may find old relationships parochial or stifling. To overcome isolation and cultural shock, you must patiently take advantage of all opportunities to widen your circle of acquaintance.

Whether you have returned or are a newcomer, there are pro-grammes designed to help you get to know mid-1990s Hong Kong.

Betty Wei in the garden at Government House in 1993, with Lavender Patten, the Governor's wife – who, like many another expat spouse gave up her (law) career to be with her husband.

The lish-Speaking Department of the YWCA in Macdonnell Road, and the American Women's Association in Kennedy Road, for instance, welcome women of all nationalities. Both organizations offer lectures, tours and how-to programmes introducing you to the Hong Kong culture, and helping you acquire skills you may always have wanted but have not been able to try – whether smocking or shadow-boxing. At least they will give you opportunities to meet women like you, newly arrived or long in residence; with luck they will enrich your sojourn with physical, social and intellectual activities.

Chinese shadow-boxing will cost you nothing, once you have learned this graceful way to fitness. Here a taichi *master teaches expatriates, in the Botanical Gardens.*

For more serious problems, there are guidance and counselling services. According to Jane Rice, a counsellor on chemical abuse who has lived here so long that she considers herself a Hong Kong person, there is no need to feel despair. You are not alone, as a majority of expatriate spouses have difficulty in adjusting to life in Hong Kong, at least during their first few months, or immediately after the exciting first stage of moving into new homes. Wives are deprived of the supporting network they enjoyed before coming to Hong Kong, while the working spouses are too preoccupied with their jobs to pay attention to domestic difficulties. The Community Advice Bureau can point the way to guidance and counselling services, such as the one at St John's Cathedral.

The Individual Without a Label

It is difficult to find a person in Hong Kong without a label. It is also difficult, although not impossible, for a person who arrives without a specific affiliation to find a place for him or herself. It took a young man from Taiwan with extremely distinguished parentage – educated in the most prestigious American schools and universities, fully competent in English and Putonghua – almost half a year to land a job (but it was a wonderful job that fully employed his talents, training, and connections). In Hong Kong, you are introduced as the son or son-in-law of Da Laoban or a grandson of Lao Taiye; or, as an expatriate with no local relatives, you will be introduced as Charles Berendsen, the Managing Director of such and such company, or as Stephen Garvin, a rising young star of the Hushuo Badao Company. It would be strange indeed if you were introduced as plain John or Joan Robinson. Trying to establish yourself as an individual is not the thing to do in Hong Kong. Your label is your legitimacy.

The Working Wife and the Filipina Maid

It is not our intention to tie the working wife to the Filipina maid concept. However these English-speaking imported domestics, many of whom are educated working wives and mothers who have left their families behind, certainly have made it possible for many Hong Kong wives and mothers to hold jobs outside the home.

Unless you are a professional, especially in finance or related services, and are bi-lingual in English and Chinese, it is difficult to find a job here. A few years ago, your fluent command of English would have been an asset, but now you will be competing with bi-lingual women with local knowledge and technical skills. Furthermore, Hong Kong is still a man's world. Few successful women here have made it on their own. Behind almost every conspicuously successful woman in Hong Kong – and fewer than a score can be put in this category – you will find the financial resources of her father or husband. Less than a handful of these women are expat wives. None of this means that you will not be able to find a job in your profession. As a newcomer, how would people know that your talents are available unless you shout them from the roof top? Seriously, this is where your networking can come in handy.

Almost all dependent husbands find jobs easily, including a deep-sea diver whose wife came as a university research student.

The Immigration Department reveals that there are more citizens of the Philippines in Hong Kong than of any other nation. An overwhelming majority of them are here as domestic workers. Whether they are called domestic servants, housekeepers, governesses, nurse-maids, household helpers, domestic helpers, maids or amahs, Filipinas have made it possible for the expatriate wife to run a home with full- or part-time help. The disadvantage is that these maids do not speak Cantonese. Their advantages are many. The Hong Kong Government's regulations on imported domestic help are clear and exact. They protect employers and employees alike, although from time to time either side may find these regulations a hindrance rather than a help.

CONCLUSION

You must find your own nook in Hong Kong. It is not a bad place once you succeed in penetrating the veneer, and can build your own *guanxi* – special relationship – with friends, shops and colleagues. After all, this is an urban community rather than a small village. It is as impersonal as large cities elsewhere. Once settled, however, you will find yourself fitting in – perhaps not exactly as if the place had been made for you – but comfortably, in your own niche.

— Chapter Four —

TRADITIONS, RELIGIONS, AND SUPERSTITIONS

Immigrants to Hong Kong brought traditions, superstitions, religious beliefs and practices from their own cultures with them. Some of the festive celebrations, such as the Lunar New Year and Christmas, have become a part of the Hong Kong heritage and are observed as public holidays. Others, like the Hindu Festival of Lights and the Jewish Rosh Hashanah, are celebrated by the particular communities but have not become a part of the general culture of Hong Kong.

FUNGSHUI

In Hong Kong, *fungshui* is taken seriously. Literally meaning 'wind and water', *fungshui* is perhaps the single most important Chinese concept that is universally embraced in Hong Kong. The English equivalent of this term is geomancy, a system of divination by means of figures or lines, but the English term is almost never used in Hong Kong. Here, *fungshui* is a household word that is understood by everyone regardless of age, gender or national root.

Fungshui masters, as practitioners are called, examine all aspects of a structure – be it a building for the living or a grave for the dead. If it is a new structure, *fungshui* considerations range from selection of the site, orientation of the building, alignment of the doors and windows, to the placing of furniture. If a building already stands, then the *fungshui* examination will consider the best way to readjust the forces in order to re-establish the natural balance and suit the demands of the owner. Good *fungshui* as an essential ingredient for any success is understood by the Hong Kong population. It is no less important in siting a grave because, in addition to ensuring peaceful rest for those buried there, it will enable them to negotiate with the powers that be to grant their progeny wealth, longevity and male heirs. Whether for topping out a building or digging a grave, auspicious dates are selected by *fungshui*.

As a metaphysical system of prophecy, *fungshui* had its origin in the *Classic of Changes*, one of the five influential texts of antiquity. The title of this work is sometimes also rendered in English as the *Book of Divination*. Its date of compilation is a matter of scholarly debate, but the work is believed to have been compiled in stages at different times. With stalks of the common yarrow plant, diviners developed a system using eight sets of three rows of whole or broken lines, as a replacement for reading cracks on bones and tortoise shells in the practice of their craft. Later the stalks were replaced by lines drawn on paper and arranged to constitute an octagon. The eight sets of trigrams, each comprising all possible arrangements of three rows of whole or broken lines, are often represented in Asian art and will no doubt be familiar to you before long.

The task for the *fungshui* master is, by interpreting the combinations of these trigrams, to choose the best *fungshui* for the specific circumstances under consideration. The *Classic of Changes* provides clues to such interpretations; so, in today's parlance, it can be called a diviner's handbook, albeit with a great deal of mystical power attached. The handbook has a number of appendices which further elaborate the metaphysical significance of these interpretations. The appendices were thought at one time to be the work of Confucius, perhaps by way of adding respectability to the book; but his authorship has been made more than doubtful by modern scholarship.

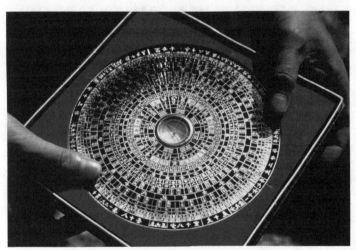

A board displaying the eight trigrams used in determining fungshui.

The *Classic of Changes* also contains a discourse on the *yin* and the *yang*, two fundamental forces which govern the creation and the working of the universe. *Yin* is the passive, negative, gentler or female principle of the universe. *Yang* is the active, positive, aggressive or male principle. Combined, the *yin* and the *yang* created the universe and made it work.

During the third century before Christ, intermingled in Taoist thinking with the *yin* and the *yang*, the system of *fungshui* began to be used more widely in the search for a balance between all elements of nature. Since that time *fungshui* has been concerned more with the working of the universe than with its creation. *Fungshui* masters must come from a well-educated background because, in addition to the *Classic of Changes* and the writings of the Taoist masters – Lao Zi (Lao Tzu) and Zhuang Zi (Chuang Tzu) – they need to be familiar with the Chinese systems of astrology and cosmology. In Hong Kong, fees for *fungshui* masters are calculated by the square foot – as the purchase price or rent for the premises will be when they appear on the market.

Actually, the practical considerations inherent in *fungshui* principles are comprehensible even to the uninitiated. In choosing the location and appointment of buildings, for instance, *fungshui* calls for the best way to make use of a given site, with fresh air and the safety of the inhabitants as top priorities. When the New Territories were added to Hong Kong in 1898, the tradition of *fungshui* was so firmly rooted among the villagers that the British administration had to heed it where possible. Chinese residents under the British administration have likewise been pragmatic. When ancestral graves gave way to modernization programmes of new towns and expressways, it was the villagers who made the compromise by making adjustments to the *fungshui*.

During the centuries since *fungshui* was first absorbed into Taoist thinking, a great deal of superstition has crept in, until today *fungshui* practices appear to encompass a lot of hocus-pocus. The land of Hong Kong is supposed to be filled with dragons – auspicious omens. Kowloon, literally meaning 'nine dragons', is so named because it is the land of eight hills. Each hill is said to be inhabited by a dragon, so there were eight dragons. The ninth dragon was added to honour the presence of an emperor who was visiting Kowloon at that time. On the Hong Kong side, Garden Road is the spine of a sprawling dragon that faces the sea. When the new Bank of China building was under construction in Garden Road, the Hong Kong Chinese were said to be displeased because the structure was reputed to be sitting on the dragon's head. It is understood that adjustments had to be made in Government House in order to compensate for the loss of good *fungshui* to the territory.

Even if you do not believe any of the *fungshui* principles and 'do not want to have anything to do with this nonsense', please remember that the people around you will be taking it extremely seriously.

In Hong Kong good luck means prosperity: arrangements must be made to ensure the best *fungshui* for home and office premises, so that a business and its owner can prosper. The best *fungshui* location faces the water with a mountain behind, an ideal not always possible in an urban community. Hence, water is brought into the premises in the form of a fish tank. Fish also deflect evil. 'Money corners' have to be found in every room through the planting of auspicious greenery and placing of lucky objects. In fact, plants are not such a bad idea since they are decorative and they bring warmth to any room, or balcony for that matter. Regardless of size, Hong Kong balconies are filled with green plants which make otherwise bleak and dirty buildings quite attractive. Mirrors are hung to deflect any ill luck that might be lurking. It can never be just any mirror placed at random. In order not to cause further deterioration in the *fungshui*, it must be a round mirror encased in an octagonal frame of eight trigrams with the correct configuration, placed under the direction of a knowledgeable *fungshui* master.

Evil spirits can be kept out of the premises by placing a screen at the entrance. While metal grid gates at the entrances of Chinese homes and offices may be a deterrent to thieves, screens just inside the doors are there to keep out intruders from the non-human world. Hong Kong's crematorium at Cape Collinson, meanwhile, contains a co-lumbarium of 19,600 niches each with capacity for two sets of ashes. The columbarium is built as an octagon, with windows resembling the eight trigrams.

CONFUCIANISM

Confucianism is not a religion because it is not concerned with a superhuman power personified by a God or gods who exact obedience and adoration. Nor is it an established system of faith and worship. Confucianism does not address the question of life after death or the issue of salvation. It is a humanist philosophy that explicates certain principles of behaviour. Confucius (born 551 BC) – coincidentally a contemporary of the Buddha, Sakyamuni (born 557 BC) – was venerated as a teacher, never as a deity. As a moral principle and a political philosophy, Confucianism has permeated Chinese thought and personal relationships as well as national regimes for more than two millennia.

TAOISM AND BUDDHISM IN HONG KONG

Taoism, also, did not begin as a religion. Intellectually it is a philosophy of withdrawal, a return to the state of nature when individuals led a simpler life free from the structures and strictures of society. Its exponents were proposing an alternative to the incessant warfare of the time, and to the rigid political system propounded by adherents of the Confucian and Legalist schools. Popular Taoism did not come until later, when traditional deities and ancestors became amalgamated into what were thought to be Taoist practices; later a body of clergy evolved.

In its popular form, Taoism can be said to be a religion. Its clergy perform important rituals such as funerals, when they chant to exorcise the evil spirits that might be present to disturb the departed as well as their families. Certain historical figures known for their special achievements were added to the Taoist pantheon of immortals. The Eight Immortals, seven men and one woman, who had been endowed with mythical values and supernatural powers, are favourites among the Taoist pantheon. They are appealed to individually or as a group; as a group they make a favourite theme in Chinese art, and crafts.

A Taoist ceremony at the water's edge. Note the yin *and* yang *sign on the boat, next to English letters. The priest's gown is embroidered with trigrams.*

Buddhism was the first all-embracing religion the Chinese had known, in the sense that the Buddha preached compassion for all living things and that Buddhism addressed the issue of salvation. It was Mahayana Buddhism, which did not demand total negation of worldly responsibilities here and now, that received popular acceptance as well as imperial patronage more than a thousand years ago. Since believers did not have to deny traditional deities or Chinese ancestors – and despite involvement by various Buddhist sects in political movements from time to time – the religion has survived, and it thrives in Hong Kong.

Being pragmatic people, Chinese Buddhists found a ready solution to the problem of vegetarianism as well. Monks, nuns and a large number of lay people were total vegetarians, but other adherents could become symbolic vegetarians. Symbolic vegetarians eat no meat on the fifteenth and the last days of the month, and they eat only vegetarian food on the first and last days of each year. Thus they

85

satisfy themselves that, at the beginning and at the end of the cycle of the moon and throughout the lunar year, they have avoided the consumption of flesh. It is curious, however, that dishes made to avoid the consumption of flesh should be called 'vegetarian pork', 'vegetarian goose', 'vegetarian shark's fin', and so forth.

Buddhist and Taoist worshippers do not gather in large congregations at prescribed times on a given day. Funeral services are religious rituals, and represent rare occasions when people need to assemble. From time to time, monks and priests are called to lead recitations of the *sutra* but, as a rule, people commune with their deities individually. Worshippers kneel in front of the altar at home or in a temple, as they ask for their wishes to be granted; and may sit as they meditate or recite the *sutra*, holding their prayer beads in their hands. It does seem incongruous to see Western-clad individuals in modern Hong Kong in such traditional postures and, under the circumstances, it would be understandable if you did not take them seriously. Since you see individuals rather than a congregation at a service when you visit a temple, it is easy to forget that they are engaged in acts of worship and not putting on a theatrical performance. In any case, please remember that it is as inconsiderate to walk between Buddhist worshippers and their altars as it is to saunter between the pews or up and down the aisle during a Christian service.

Taoist and Buddhist Temples in Hong Kong

When a temple in Hong Kong is identified as a *miao* or a *shi*, it is usually Buddhist. When it is called a *kuan*, it is always Taoist. But you should not be surprised to find all manner of images crossing religious lines. Not counting street and private altars in shops and homes, there are almost four hundred Buddhist and Taoist temples in Hong Kong, including a number which are older than the colony. Chinese temples are where spirits of the deities reside, although only their earthen or wooden images are visible. In Hong Kong, temples are also repositories of spiritual tablets, wooden plaques on which names of the

Worshippers of all ages in a temple at the Lunar New Year.

ancestors whose spirits reside there were inscribed. In the native places, these plaques were placed in the ancestral halls, and there are still ancestral halls remaining in the New Territories. Temples in Hong Kong are rarely great monuments of architecture, and few contain valuable works of art. Though they welcome visitors, they are places of worship and pilgrimage, not solely tourist sites.

Ching Chung Koon (Green Pine Temple) is a Taoist temple built in 1949 near Castle Peak in northwest New Territories. It is dedicated to Lui Cho (nicknamed Lü Dongbing), one of the Eight Immortals, and two of his followers. Lui was born in 755 AD and served as a magistrate in what is now Jiangxi. After successfully overcoming ten temptations, he was singled out to be taught certain skills by the first of the Eight Immortals – whose existence was probably mythical rather than historical. Lui was elevated to the status of an immortal after travelling throughout the empire slaying devils, for a period reported in some accounts to be as long as four centuries. Taoist dating is similar to that of the Old Testament, sometimes difficult for human minds to fathom. From the twelfth century onwards, the Chinese populace began to construct temples in Lui's honour. The Hong Kong temple boasts a respectable library and a wonderful collection of *bonsai* trees, some with topiary work.

The Wong Tai Sin Temple in Kowloon, erected in 1973 on the site of an older Wong Tai Sin Temple built in 1921, stands as a reminder that religious fervour had not dwindled in Hong Kong despite modernization and preoccupation with the amassing of money. Situated amidst the splendour and squalor of urban Kowloon, it is a large complex of buildings honouring a host of Buddhist and Taoist deities. The chief object of adoration here is the popular Taoist personage Wong Tai Sin. Wong lived in the coastal province of Zhejiang and developed an elixir of good health and eternal life. Given the *soubriquet* Tai Sin, 'Great Ethereal Spirit', Wong is venerated as a healer. It is important for people in Hong Kong to be assured of good health so that they may pursue whatever tasks they choose. Asking divine assistance is like buying more insurance, hence the popularity of the temple.

The outbuildings of the temple contain shops handling many varieties of merchandise, from religious images and incense and paper currency for the underworld, to stalls for fortune-tellers. Hong Kong people living abroad continue to send their friends and relatives to the fortune-tellers at the Wong Tai Sin Temple for their services on major occasions, say to name a new baby or ascertain the astrological compatibility of a couple intending to marry. To avoid confusion in case the intermediaries fail to pass on the exact message word for word, the fortune-tellers have adopted a modern means of communication: the tape recorder.

The Man Mo Temple in Hollywood Road, the first temple built on Hong Kong Island after the arrival of the British, was dedicated to the God of Literature (Man) and the God of War (Wu). Also within the temple was the Buddhist Bodhisattva Guanyin, popularly translated as the Goddess of Mercy, among whose attributes was the provision of male heirs.

GODDESS OF THE SEA OR QUEEN OF HEAVEN

In a community dependent upon the water, the Goddess of the Sea and protector of those who sail on the waters enjoys an imposing edifice to house her image. This deity, now called Tin Hou (Queen of Heaven) in Hong Kong, was venerated by the seafaring population all along the Chinese coast. You may find at least two dozen Tin Hou temples; some are small but most of them are splendid structures. The most impressive Tin Hou temples in Hong Kong are at Aberdeen, Repulse Bay, Yaumatei, and Joss House Bay – not necessarily on the water's edge, though, after massive land reclamation since their construction. Certain occasions, such as Tin Hou's birthday, are still celebrated in Hong Kong by the fisher folk and seafarers, with sounds and pageantry.

CHRISTIANS

It was difficult for a Chinese to be converted to Christianity: because of its monotheistic character and because early missionaries were bent on getting rid of the tradition which they termed 'ancestor worship', but which the Chinese had held to be important for several thousand years. Believing in pre-determination by fate, that one's destiny was prescribed from birth, the Chinese were not ready to accept the concepts of original sin and salvation through Jesus Christ. Early Jesuit missionaries were noted as purveyors of such Western technology as the calendar, astronomy and firearms to the Ming and Qing courts – but not for any large-scale successes in converting Chinese souls. After the Opium War, Roman Catholic and Protestant missionaries were active in proselytizing, as well as in modernizing the Chinese curriculum, but the people did not flock to the religion.

The first Roman Catholic mission in Hong Kong was founded in 1841. Today, the Roman Catholic Diocese, established in 1946, has over sixty parishes with more than a quarter of a million communicants, or about five per cent of the Hong Kong population. Protestant missionaries were active in Canton and came to Hong Kong in 1841. They usurped the term *Christian* for their exclusive use, hence 'Christian church' in Hong Kong denotes a Protestant place of worship. Today, there are at least 870 Protestant churches, with 258,000 members belonging to more than fifty denominations. There is an Anglican cathedral, but the tremendous growth of Protestantism is due to the evangelical zeal of lay Chinese Christians. You may find a congenial church, because Hong Kong Christians are friendly and welcoming; but, if you do not understand Cantonese, your choice is limited. Not every denomination is represented here, but you will for example find a Christian Scientist and a small Quaker congregation. The larger congregations and parishes tend to be ecumenical. There are separate services in Mandarin and in Tagalog, a language of the Philippines. There are also Korean-language congregations.

Friends celebrating Christmas. Note the absence of the generations now overseas.

Christmas in Hong Kong

Christmas is a public holiday, celebrated by the entire population each in his own way. Hong Kong takes on a festive air for the entire month of December and into January, when preparations for the Lunar New Year begin. Christmas is a two-day holiday thanks to the English tradition of celebrating the day after Christmas, 26 December, as Boxing Day. The buildings along the Victoria and Kowloon water-fronts are aglow with neon brilliance. The decorations are not merely Christmas trees and colourful lights, they are large scenes depicting themes of Chinese and Western folklore. Restaurants and shops which are not normally closed on Sundays stay open during the Christmas holidays. Hotels offer traditional Western Christmas fare – food and music. Motor traffic is kept away, to enable pedestrians to enjoy the festive scenes on foot in Central and Tsimshatsui.

To many Hong Kong Chinese, Christmas has joined the Lunar New Year as an occasion for gift giving. With glaring lights and blaring music, Christmas in Hong Kong has become as tinselled and commercialized as some of the most secular you might have left behind. Merchants with a keen sense for opportunities to make a fast dollar, were quick to promote Santa Claus as the moving spirit of Christmas celebrations. This is also the time for charity donations through the sale of greeting cards, and parties for handicapped children and indigent elderly. In this respect, the public celebration of Christmas in Hong Kong differs little from the genre you probably know. Being able to celebrate one more holiday in such style further reflects the economic well-being of a segment of the Hong Kong population. It also shows Western influences institutionalized by the commercial sector of Hong Kong.

Christmas shopping, under the eye of a foreign Immortal.

However, in another sense, Christmas celebrations in Hong Kong are like nothing you have seen before. Instead of attending a church service and a family gathering, you may mark the birth of the Christ Child, Hong Kong style, at one of the myriad restaurant-nightclubs on Christmas Eve and Christmas morning. If you really cannot suppress an urge to experience such an evening for yourself, be prepared for a unique awakening. You will marvel at the restaurateur's originality in incorporating elements from Western celebrations of New Year's Eve, by providing noise-makers and party-hats with the delicious dinner. What may compel you to abort the evening will be the band's thunderous rendering of *Hark! The Herald Angels Sing* and *Silent Night* in rock 'n' roll rhythm – to which you will be expected to swing, and sing along too no doubt, with the karaoke machine.

CHINESE FESTIVALS

Five Chinese festivals are marked by public holidays in Hong Kong: the Lunar New Year, the Ching Ming Festival, the Dragon Boat Festival, the Mid-Autumn Festival, and Chung Yeung. Ching Ming is a time for remembering, and at Chung Yeung people climb to higher ground, an excuse to spend some time out of doors with the family; in Hong Kong it is also an occasion to visit ancestral graves. The other festivals are joyous occasions marked by great ceremonies and special foods.

The Lunar New Year, like Easter, is a movable feast. It is the most significant of the Chinese festivals, and is the most elaborately celebrated. Until after the mid-1980s, offices, schools, factories, shops and restaurants were closed for at least five days, some for as many as fifteen, because this was the time of the annual vacation for workers. In recent years, one or two restaurants have even opened on the first day of the New Year, and a large number are opening on the second or third day, probably to earn extra money to cover their overheads. Conservative employers, especially in cases when workers do not even take Sundays off, still allow their hirelings a more extensive respite for the holiday season. With the advent of Filipina domestic help, Hong Kong's household services, at least, no longer come to a complete halt – as they did when Chinese amahs used to return to their native villages and not re-emerge until the end of the month.

A father helping his child choose a lantern for the Mid-Autumn Festival.

The buildings on both sides of the harbour are again neon-lit, but the greetings are now changed to 'Felicitations and Prosperity', more suitable to the Chinese New Year season and the Hong Kong ethos. The population, the children at least, don bright-coloured clothing and enter into the spirit of the holiday. There are special dishes for the New Year, and the most conspicuous decorations in Hong Kong are the miniature orange trees and flowering peach branches which are everywhere. No unlucky word is supposed to be uttered; children are fed sweets constantly, to mollify the ill effect of any unfortunate word that might emerge from their mouths.

The nicest aspect of the Lunar New Year celebrations in Hong Kong is the firework display on the second day of the year. Three boats are moored in the harbour. Wonderful fireworks are shot into the night sky, synchronized with music specially composed for the occasion. Usually, a major company will sponsor this much awaited event. All traffic along the harbour stops during the display, and hundreds of thousands of the populace line the shore and the roads, uttering the ubiquitous 'Wah' each time anything rises from the boats. Nobody has yet made any comment about the political implications of the red stars soaring above the still British territory. If you rent a hotel room with a harbour view in order to watch the display, do not count on leaving until well after the roads are reopened.

The single most important ritual for you to remember is to wish everyone 'Fat choy'. This concept, of gaining a large amount of money during the coming year, has become an integral part of the season's ritual. You hand out red *laisee* packets. You give one to everyone you see, almost: your household, the people who normally

Children receiving laisee *at Chinese New Year's. Note the peach blossoms and the miniature golden orange tree.*

render you services such as the doormen in your apartment and office buildings, all the children you meet, and all the unmarried adults too. The office as well as household staff normally draw a thirteenth month's pay at this time, but you must not forget to give each a red packet on the first working day of the year. The amount in each envelope depends on your relationship to the recipient; bear in mind, though, that all paper currency feels the same inside a paper packet. So, unless you use different designs for the differing amounts inside, you will find yourself in a confused state of mind each time you hand out a *laisee*. To make the distinction even more evident, you can insert the same amount in each envelope and simply hand one to some people and more than one to others. Children used to be happy with anything, and indeed they are spoilt by the large number of *laisee* gifts they receive these days. The Hong Kong streets are littered with discarded red packets, while the bolder children sing the jingle 'Felicitations and Prosperity! *Laisee* is coming my way. I really do not want any that contain only one dollar, but I will welcome any packet with a ten dollar bill inside.' Inflation, we understand, has raised the ante of the children's disclaimer to 'ten dollars' and the minimum welcomed to 'one hundred'.

Grave Sweeping at Ching Ming

The Chinese commemorate their departed progenitors by visiting family shrines and sweeping ancestral graves, at Ching Ming in early spring. In Hong Kong, residents whose ancestral graves are not in the territory head for their home villages in a mass exodus to China.

Like other traditions, this practice of commemorating the dead has undergone many changes inside China. It has been declared superstitious by twentieth century reformers, and eradicated as an opiate of the people by Maoist modernizers; but these traditions have been faithfully observed outside China wherever there are large concentrations of ethnic Chinese from a bygone era. Southeast Asia, including Hong Kong, has become a rich repository of old Chinese traditions.

At ancestral graves in Hong Kong. Hillside positions optimize fungshui. *Food, incense and flowers are offered. Photographs of the buried are baked into porcelain and set on the headstone.*

Newcomers soon attune themselves, and flock back to family graves in China at Ching Ming and other weekends.

The tradition of honouring the dead means offering obeisance and food in front of the spiritual tablets housed in family shrines; or, in the absence of such tablets today, before photographs of departed progenitors. The offerings are symbolic gestures to the ancestors to ensure that they continue to enjoy their sustenance in the nether world. Similar ceremonies are performed at the grave-side. Incense sticks are lit. Cooked cold food is offered and, here in Hong Kong, there is always a roast pig. For some reason that nobody could remember even during the seventeenth century, no fire is lit in the kitchen at Ching Ming. Pieces of paper folded into shapes resembling silver and gold ingots are burned in furnaces in the temples, since fires are no longer allowed in the cemeteries. Today, on the assumption that inflation is

97

not confined to this world, paper currency in $1,000,000 denominations is sent to the ancestors – also through the flames.

Dragon Boat Races

The Tuen Ng Festival takes place at the beginning of the summer, when the weather in North China is just warm enough for outdoor sports. It is marked in Hong Kong by dragon boat races, promoted by the Hong Kong Tourist Association into an international event. The races were a tradition of fishermen and boatmen of the rivers. The noisy dragon boats and glutinous rice buns, associated with this festival, are said to have originated during the third century BC by the local people to save the poet and official Qu Yuan from the fish in the Milo River. Qu had thrown himself into the river when he became despondent because his sovereign had not heeded his entreaties to rid the kingdom of corruption. With the drummer beating the rhythm and oarsmen rowing with all their might, the races have embraced participants from all sectors of Hong Kong. This is an occasion for

Dragon boat racing in Hong Kong waters; reviving a traditional way to celebrate Duanwu.

expatriates and locals to play together. There are men's and women's teams. On another day, there are participants from other Asian countries as well.

Chung Yeung Festival in Hong Kong

This holiday is celebrated in Hong Kong on the ninth day of the ninth lunar month, when people climb the highest hill they can find or care to ascend. The legend of 'mounting the heights', dating from no earlier than the Han dynasty, celebrates the number nine. It concerns a fortune-teller who warned a virtuous scholar of an impending calamity and told him to take his family to the mountains for the day. When the scholar and his family returned in the evening, they found that disaster had indeed struck, and that all his livestock had died. Time went on and nobody paid much attention to this holiday, except for scholars; they went up into the mountains, drank, and perhaps flew kites. Along the Yangzi River, it was a holiday only for tailors. Families which retained the services of tailors gave them the day off, and treated them to a banquet with chrysanthemum wine.

Somehow, in Hong Kong, early Chinese settlers convinced the British administration that this was an important festival. Perhaps it came from a legend of the Song dynasty connected with Tin Hou. Tin Hou was supposed to have been born in 960 AD; though descended from generations of well-known public officials, her father had chosen to live among simple fishermen on a small island off the Chinese coast. Tin Hou's birth was said to have been unusual: her mother, a devout Buddhist, had a dream during which the Bodhisattva Guanyin provided her with a pill; afterwards Tin Hou was born. At the age of seven she was showing exceptional intelligence. When she was thirteen a visiting monk, impressed by her unique qualities, taught her the secrets of transmigration of the soul. At Chung Yeung in the year 986, when all in China climbed to high ground, Tin Hou was said to have ascended higher and higher until she merged with the sky. From there she made appearances and saved fishermen and other sailors from death among the waves. She is much venerated in Macau.

For the populace of Hong Kong, Chung Yeung is another opportunity to visit ancestral graves.

HONG KONG WEDDINGS

Hong Kong marriages may be made in heaven, but weddings are definitely earthly affairs. Not every couple's dates and times of birth are vetted by fortune-tellers nowadays, but the astrological calendar is still consulted for an auspicious date. The wedding itself is not a religious rite, but there is a ritual to the occasion. Most weddings take place in the Marriage Registry, to which you would not expect to be invited. However you will probably be invited to the wedding banquet of every one of your colleagues who ties the knot during your time here, and very likely to those of their relations as well. These banquets are neither intimate nor exclusive affairs. The larger the banquet, the more face the bride and groom, or their parents, will garner. Literally hundreds of people are invited. Unless you are out of town, you must accept the invitation and attend the banquet. There will be very few Westerners present, but you will be seated with people you know.

There is no such thing as not being able to afford to put on a wedding banquet. Everyone brings a cash gift – in a red packet, of course – or you can buy a redeemable gift certificate from a bank, which the bridal couple can exchange for cash. The amount depends on your connection with the bridal couple, but should certainly not be less than a good meal would cost for two people. Always give an even number of notes as well as dollar amounts – two hundred, six hundred, one thousand, two thousand; never an odd number – three hundred, five hundred, or nine hundred. In theory, it is the parents of the groom who foot the bill because they are the hosts of this feast celebrating their acquisition of a daughter-in-law, the mother of their future grandsons. In fact, depending on the financial circumstances of the families, the cash gifts help. Modern brides from families with no financial constraint have taken to registering their 'wedding lists' at local shops, but nobody objects to cash.

The wedding banquet takes place in a large, and therefore noisy, restaurant. There will be a photographer, who takes pictures of everybody posing with the bride and the groom, and as many candid shots as they can muster. Since everybody will be playing mahjong or card games, including the people from your office, you will not want to arrive early. This will be an extremely noisy gathering, because it is a good time to have friends and colleagues together in a relaxed non-office atmosphere. Everybody is supposed to be having a good time, and having a good time means making a lot of noise. While it is rude to bring your needlework or your laptop computer to while away the three or four hours before dinner is served, it is not impolite to time your arrival to the start of dinner.

At the banquet table you will see a bottle of brandy, and perhaps a bottle of Scotch whisky, and sweet soda pop in tins. At Hong Kong wedding banquets wine, especially champagne, seems to be reserved for the bridal table. While food is being consumed, the bride will change her clothes twice – from the rented Western wedding gown, to a traditional Chinese dress, to a Western evening dress, perhaps also rented for the day. The bride and the groom will go from table to table to toast their guests. As soon as dessert is served, which normally consists of Chinese sweet cakes and oranges – symbolizing many sons because, until the advent of Sunkist, oranges contained many seeds – the bride and the groom, with his parents, will be standing at the restaurant door to wish you a good night. There is no need to linger after the feast is finished.

Should the celebration be modern as distinct from traditional, a cocktail reception is held in a hotel or a club. If the marriage is between a Chinese and a non-Chinese, the scene is strangely revealing. You will see the Chinese guests attacking the food, while the Westerners home in on the booze.

A part of the wedding ceremony you will not be invited to witness, is when the new bride serves tea to all the senior members of the

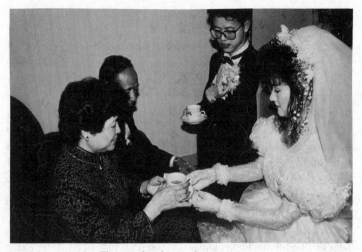

The new daughter-in-law serving tea.

husband's family – that is, any one who is older than her husband. Relatives are served in rigid order of seniority; this order also determines the amount a person will give to the new bride as *laisee*, or lucky money. Junior members are to give a smaller *laisee* than the senior members so as not to be perceived to outshine the seniors. This social etiquette is clearly defined for other occasions as well.

HONG KONG FUNERALS

Funerals are important occasions in Hong Kong, as well. They are usually held in one of the two large funeral emporia, one on Hong Kong Island and the other in Kowloon. However, despite the sometimes overlong wait for space to become available, even Christian services are seldom held in church.

A grand send-off gives tremendous face to the deceased and the family. You attend the service to pay your respects to a friend or a colleague, and you assume that everybody else is there for the same reason. However this, like other Hong Kong occasions, can be used by people to show other people that they and the departed were on intimate terms; but only if the departed was a person of social significance. The size of the attendance at a funeral is in direct proportion to the wealth and fame of the deceased, or of his sons. The placement of the wreaths, and the names of their donors, prominently shown for all to see, make interesting reading while you wait for the ritual to begin.

There is a set of rules for funeral services. Send a floral tribute ahead of time, although the practice of donating to charities instead of squandering on wreaths is beginning to catch on in Hong Kong. Ask your Chinese friends and colleagues whether you should opt for the latter. If they say nothing, send flowers. Wear dark clothing, preferably black, to the service. Do not worry about what to do once you get there. There will be professional funeral directors to give you specific instructions in English. Be prepared, however, to walk towards the deceased at the end of the hall and bow to the photograph of the deceased. The casket will not be wheeled in until the service has begun. It will be open. At some time during the service, the mourners are expected to walk round the casket to say farewell to the deceased. You can seat yourself away from the centre of the hall if you do not wish to circumnavigate the coffin.

You will be given a small white envelope which will contain a coin and a piece of sweet. The coin is a symbolic gesture to help defray the cost of your car fare to the funeral. The sweet is to help lessen your sadness. Sometimes there is also a white washcloth or handkerchief to help wipe away your tears. You can eat the sweet as you leave the service and pocket the coin. Do whatever you wish with the washcloth or the handkerchief. There is no etiquette governing its disposal. Remember: funerals always start on time, and there is no parking.

Christian funerals are like similar services that you know at home. Buddhist or Taoist services, on the other hand, are interesting to an outside observer. Eulogies and other laudatory remarks are not a part of the Buddhist or Taoist funeral rite because they concern the worldly achievements of the deceased, which are not important after he is dead. The presence of monks at a Buddhist funeral, and the rites that comprise chanting of *sutras*, burning of incense, and recitation of prayers, are to aid the transmigration of his soul. Your presence is sufficient to comfort the bereaved family. Unless you know the family well, there is no need to say anything to them at all. A simple bow will suffice.

LUCKY SYMBOLS AND NUMBERS

In the Chinese language, many characters, as Chinese words are called, have the same sound. There are 26 letters in the English alphabet, but 214 radicals with which to compose the Chinese characters. For instance, *two*, *to*, and *too* sound alike but each word has a different meaning, completely unrelated to its homonyms; similarly *lesson* and *lessen*. But homonyms in the Chinese language are more numerous than in English. Sometimes more than a score of characters can have the same sound; different tones, maybe, but the same sound. No less a personage than Professor Lu Bisong, retired head of the Beijing Languages Institute and Chairman of International Chinese Language Teaching Association, reports that the largest number of homonymous characters in the language is 61.

In Hong Kong, words, and numbers also, take on special significance when they sound like something auspicious. Whether or not one approves of such superstitions, it is the practice to take as much luck as you can. The word meaning 'bat', for instance, is pronounced *fu*, which is a homonym for 'good luck' – as in *fu* of '*fu* (good luck), *lu* (good luck in the sense of a career), and *shou* (long life)', the three classically dressed porcelain figures you see in every restaurant and shop in Hong Kong. Hence you find bats painted on dishes, woven into scarves, and everywhere else as well. *Chang zhou* (long life) is used to greet a living person, wishing her or him many years on this planet. *Yun zhou* (eternal life), on the other hand, is a term used only for the dead who are already enjoying life somewhere else for eternity. *Yu* , fish, is a homonym for *plenty*. Especially at the last meal before the Lunar New Year, fish is always served but, in theory at least, never consumed. This is to symbolize the plenty that is left over from year to year. So, if you are a guest at a Lunar New Year's Eve dinner at a restaurant, do not touch the fish unless your host puts it on your plate. Even then, watch to see whether he eats his portion first.

Chinese fortune-telling: in Western dress.

There are many more examples showing how luck is important in Hong Kong. The colour red, for instance, symbolizes happiness; therefore red is a lucky colour. White is the colour of mourning. That is why for auspicious occasions, such as birthdays, weddings, and certainly the Lunar New Year, cash gifts are encased in red envelopes, never white. Butterflies symbolize marital bliss; and mandarin ducks, which always come in pairs, symbolize conjugal happiness and fidelity. Avoid wearing a green hat under all circumstances: it denotes a cuckold. Never give time-pieces as presents since 'clock' in Chinese sounds the same as 'end', translated as 'death' and 'demise'. Oranges are always good gifts because their colour symbolizes gold, and the large number of pits (seeds) inside symbolizes many sons. When visiting a sick Shanghainese-speaking friend, do not bring apples. 'Apple' is a homonym for 'death from illness' in the Shanghainese dialect – and the term 'governor', as in the Governor of Hong Kong, sounds like 'stupid idiot'.

Besides their penchant for certain words, the Hong Kong Chinese are partial to particular numbers. The number eight is *fa* in Cantonese, and hence is venerated because it sounds just like 'amassing'. What is being amassed? Money, of course – need you ask? Eight is a lucky number, so are 88, double luck, 888, triple luck, and 8888, multiple luck. But this not the whole story. Nine in Cantonese sounds like 'sufficient', so it is also desirable. Any combination of eight and nine will automatically mean amassing money until you are full to the brim. The Hong Kong Government, fully cognizant of this notion, auctions off car licence plates bearing such numbers each time a new series is issued. The world's highest price for a motor car number plate, five million Hong Kong dollars, was paid for licence number eight at an auction. The number three, which sounds like 'life', is popular as well. The number four, considered the most lucky number along the Yangzi, sounds like 'death' in Cantonese; so it is to be avoided wherever possible.

CONCLUSION

The prevailing cultural traditions, superstitions and religions that you will see here are mostly derived from the Chinese and the British. The chances are that you will not find all of these celebrations completely strange; and, through understanding the background of each tradition, superstition or religious practice a little better, you will find yourself participating in Hong Kong ceremonies with sensitivity – and enjoying colleagues' celebrations with gusto.

— *Chapter Five* —

INFORMATION, COMMUNICATION AND TRAVEL

Many factors have made it possible for Hong Kong to enjoy its international position today. In addition to the presence of capital, labour, ingenious and daring entrepreneurship, and a political climate that supports *laissez-faire* capitalism, Hong Kong boasts a strong infrastructure, including highly efficient communication and transport systems which give instant access and rapid movement to all corners of the world. Freedom of the press, a printing industry and a large reading public maintain a copious flow of information.

TELECOMMUNICATION
The moderate monthly fee allowing the subscriber an unlimited

number of local calls of any duration makes home telephones commonplace in Hong Kong. Government statistics show sixty-five telephones for every hundred residents. When you count the number of instruments in your home and office, you may not feel that this ratio is impressive. However, the total number of telephones is 3.8 million, served by 3 million exchange lines. It is worth noting that the majority of the Hong Kong population is frugal, and usually there is not more than one telephone for each household. In this age of coloured telephones and push-button technology, you would be surprised to find how many of these single-instrument households still use a black telephone with a dial.

At the other end of the scale, Hong Kong business people and residents racked up 2,522 million minutes of overseas calls in 1993, a twenty-five per cent rise from 2,025 million minutes in 1992. International Direct Dialling is available to 210 countries, and to more than 1,000 cities in China. During the hours of least telephone traffic the rates are cheaper. Please remember that there is a difference of eight hours between Hong Kong and London, thirteen between Hong Kong and New York, sixteen between Hong Kong and the West Coast, one hour the other way between Hong Kong and Tokyo, and two hours between Hong Kong and Sydney, so traffic is fairly heavy during most of the day. Cheaper rates only apply between midnight and seven in the morning, when topmost on the minds of intelligent people is not saving a few dollars on overseas telephone calls. As a result, your urge to speak to family and friends back home will be curbed considerably when you receive your first overseas telephone bill from Hong Kong Telecommunications.

The Fax

Instant communication by facsimile transmission – fax – on the other hand, is possible at all hours of the day. Fax machines can be bought at reasonable prices. Installation involves plugging the instrument into a telephone socket and a powerpoint. Not every Hong Kong home is yet equipped with fax, but there were 228,000 fax lines at the end of July 1993. These did not include machines connected to lines with *telephone* numbers; nor did it include fax-telephones. It is not the cost that keeps people from installing their fax on a *dedicated fax line* instead of a telephone line; rather, it is to avoid the nuisance of unwanted advertisements. It costs the advertisers nothing to send sales 'literature' locally, but it exhausts the recipient's fax paper. Efforts are being made to stop this electronic junk mail – which is not unconnected with the system of not charging local calls individually. Perhaps Hong Kong will follow the example of other major cities, where the system has been abandoned.

Fax has changed business communication in Hong Kong. Fewer messengers are needed to deliver letters and documents by hand. For overseas communication, it is even more of a boon. A fax is a written record while a telephone conversation is not. Although Hong Kong's Post Office is efficient, postal services at the receiving end may not be so speedy. An airmail letter from Hong Kong takes two days to reach Beijing, three days to arrive at an address in London or Frankfurt, a week to reach New York City, and up to eighteen days before delivery in the Philadelphia suburb of Bryn Mawr. A fax gets your message across instantly. There is an increasing number of international courier companies in Hong Kong, delivering documents, newspapers, magazines, books and other goods. They are competitive but, inevitably, expensive. Their pleasant, efficient telephone voices may not warn you that companies neither collect nor deliver at weekends or on public holidays. So, if you only want to send a few sheets of paper instead of a pile of unfading documents, you use the fax.

Mobile Telephones and Pagers

The very high cost of mobile telephones in Hong Kong came down after March 1993, when the monopoly of licensed operators ended; but they are still expensive. The mobile telephone is now an essential feature of Hong Kong's daily existence. As the highest per capita users, Hong Kong people probably come closest to being on the go constantly, twenty-four hours a day and seven days a week; and the stress in their lives is enormous.

Even now the cost of purchase and installation of the instrument, and by the minute when the telephone is in use, puts this means of communication beyond the reach (for example) of independent craftsmen who depend on telephone calls for their livelihood. These men, and employees of larger firms, use radio pagers. At the end of 1992, there were 1,042,000 pagers in Hong Kong, or one for every 5.6 residents, representing a spectacular increase from the year before when there were 700,000, or one pager for every eight residents. In 1993, according to the latest statistics, 1,254,000 pagers were in use – one for every 4.7 people. This method of communication may not be instant, but it is efficient. With the caller's telephone number indicated on the screen of his radio pager, only a few minutes usually pass before he can return the call. 'Time is money': another adage seemingly coined for Hong Kong.

PUBLISHING AND PRINTING

Hong Kong is proud of the freedom of its press, which underpins the strength of the publishing and printing industry in the territory. Government business registrations and labour statistics reveal that in 1993 there were 4,820 printing establishments employing 40,918 workers. Book publishing is mostly in Chinese, but English-language and bi-lingual Chinese/English publishing also thrive. There has been no effective labour union to impede the transition from manual to electronic control of setting and printing, and there is no shortage of expat spouses with editing experience, so the production of books and periodicals is relatively cost-efficient. In addition, the local printers' dual-language capability attracts major international academic publishers, such as Oxford University Press, to establish editorial and production offices in Hong Kong. Together with the local university presses, a large body of respectable scholarly and general works on China, Hong Kong and Asia at large, have been produced at fairly reasonable prices.

There are more than a million children in elementary and secondary schools in Hong Kong. Assume that every child uses at least one set of books in each category of subjects: reading, writing, arithmetic, mathematics, computer studies, general science, earth science, environment, civics, history, geography, biology, chemistry, physics, Chinese language, Chinese literature, English language, English literature – recognise that each set will have at least two volumes plus workbooks and related aids – and now add Chinese dictionaries, English dictionaries and bi-lingual dictionaries: the number of school books published each year leaves one groping for a mental abacus.

Popular non-fiction and fiction books are published, chiefly for the substantial Chinese-language readership.

The Press

Freedom of the press in Hong Kong means that there is no censorship before a newspaper or periodical is printed, but offending publications can be seized at newsstands. Journalists continue to complain that they do not enjoy complete access to Government information. In 1993, 77 newspapers and 619 periodicals were published.

Three English-language daily newspapers are *South China Morning Post*, *Hong Kong Standard* and *Eastern Express*; this last began to publish in February 1994. These newspapers benefit from regional and overseas circulation, too, as emigrants from Hong Kong try to keep in touch with what is going on here. The *Standard* publishes a Chinese edition, while the *Post* owns a Chinese daily. *Eastern Express* is owned by the Chinese-language *Oriental Daily*. If you subscribe to one of these newspapers via a telephone call to the circulation department, the paper is delivered to the lobby of your apartment block, while a subscription through the local news agent brings the paper to your door.

The Asian Wall Street Journal (the Asian edition of *The Wall Street Journal*) is published in Hong Kong. *International Herald Tribune* comes in by satellite from Paris every morning and is printed here. The *Financial Times* is printed in Japan, flown to Hong Kong and available next day. Twenty-six of the Chinese-language newspapers cover general news. Others satisfy special-interest readers such as finance and horse racing, but since these interests are general in Hong Kong, these newspapers enjoy a wide circulation.

The number of newspapers has remained fairly steady during the past decade, but there has been a tremendous growth in periodicals. There were 69 newspapers and 439 periodicals in 1982; 68 newspapers and 577 periodicals five years later in 1987; 64 newspaper and 603 periodicals in 1991. Two Hong Kong based magazines have Asia as their focus – *Far Eastern Economic Review*, in the same format as *The Economist*; and *Asiaweek*, in the same format as *Time* and *Newsweek*. *Time* and *Newsweek* publish Hong Kong editions.

A newsvendor in Central, with Chinese and English newspapers and magazines.

A casual glance at any local newsstand reveals a large variety of magazines catering to special interests including cooking, computer and electronic technology, motor cars, music, the arts and antiques, film stars, Cantopop stars, lifestyles of the rich and the famous, *kungfu* and the martial arts including Ninja, astrology, horse racing and betting, as well as serious political and social commentaries such as *Zeng Ming*. Underneath the pile of respectable publications, there are what used to be called girlie magazines, in English and in Chinese, profusely and lewdly illustrated. Newsstands offering such publications usually also handle pornographic video tapes.

Publications deemed pornographic are taken away when the police decide to enforce anti-pornographic legislation. Sometimes the publisher is fined and ordered to stop marketing the offending magazine, but it is not difficult for it to re-emerge under a different name. For this reason, and because some magazines are insufficiently funded and do not survive more than a few issues, the number of periodicals in Hong Kong remains more constant than the list of their titles.

Foreign Correspondents

The importance of Hong Kong in the international arena is reflected by the presence of a large body of foreign correspondents, representing the world's leading newspapers and periodicals. The Foreign Correspondents' Club has a roster of 325 active correspondent members and 168 journalist members. Major news agencies, including Associated Press, Reuters, United Press International, Agence France-Presse, Kyodo News Service of Japan, Agencia EFE of Spain, and LUSA of Portugal, have offices here.

The Xinhua News Agency (The New China News Agency), maintains an office with a large staff in Hong Kong; but it is more than a news agency, it is the unofficial presence of the government of the People's Republic of China. The American Dow Jones Company owns a publishing company here, which produces mainly financial journals such as *Far Eastern Economic Review* and *The Asian Wall Street Journal*. It also operates news wire and computer data retrieval services. So does Reuters.

Booksellers

Two reasons for the high price of books in Hong Kong are rents and the cost of shipping books in from abroad. Perhaps, as a compensation, the service in the English-language bookshops, such as the Hong Kong Book Centre, and Kelly and Walsh, is good. The staff know their merchandise, and will order books not in stock. There are many other bookshops handling books on the region, and world-wide pulp fiction. Times Publishing of Singapore operates a string of bookshops, as does *South China Morning Post*.

The larger Chinese-language bookshops, the Commercial Press in Causeway Bay and Joint Publishing in Central, also market English-language books. You are allowed to browse for as long as you wish and read to your heart's content. Elsewhere, alas, the Chinese practice of reading while browsing through the bookshops is a thing of the past. Books on display are wrapped in cellophane; considering the price of books in Hong Kong, who can blame the sellers? The Commercial Press also boasts a marvellous selection of stationery in its basement, but the service can best be described as indifferent.

Libraries

The Urban Council libraries are open to the public. To obtain borrowing rights, all you need is your Hong Kong Identity Card. For up-to-date information there is the American Library, a reference library operated by the United States Information Agency. Since space is limited, only researchers using the library's materials are admitted. You cannot just walk in and read your newspaper. The Library has video tapes, computerized data and reference books in all fields – plus periodicals and American newspapers including the Sunday *New York Times,* but no dailies. Reference help can also be obtained by telephone, but you need to go in person in order to watch last week's professional football games on tape. Private libraries belonging to clubs are open to members only. The Helena May (Garden Road) boasts a superb collection of children's books. The university libraries are not open to the public, but research scholars can always gain access through faculty members.

RADIO AND TELEVISION

If you are a radio listener or a television couch potato, there is plenty on the local stations to keep you diverted.

Several radio stations cater between them to all tastes from classical music to current events, Cantopop and up-to-date stockmarket prices. If you are addicted to what goes on in the pop world at home, do not despair. Such broadcasts are transmitted here with no time gap.

The standard of local television programmes is a question of personal judgement. During the recent past, the number of English-language programmes has declined, because audience demand is increasingly for other languages. Presentation that used to be in English is increasingly bi-lingual, in English and Cantonese. It is not having two languages in the same programme that annoys, so much as the pronunciation of English with a Cantonese accent and *vice versa*. Each of the two local television stations, ATV and TVB, broadcasts through two channels, one in Cantonese and the other (partly, at least) in English. The CBS Evening News comes in the early morning on one of the English-language channels. However, English-language broadcasting time is being usurped by programmes in such languages as Japanese, Korean, and Putonghua: further indications that non-English and non-Cantonese speakers are on the rise in Hong Kong.

Satellite television and cable television have invaded Hong Kong's peace of mind; but the quality of the reception varies by location, and the quality of the programmes is another matter. For English-speaking viewers, what used to be available on two channels can now be received on four; but there is no improvement in what they see. The satellite sports channel, when in English, is satisfactory; but for tennis, at least, there is a need for a commentator who speaks better Putonghua.

More than ninety-eight per cent of Hong Kong households own at least one television set, and sixty-nine per cent own VCR or laser disc equipment. The most popular programmes are the soap operas and variety shows on the Cantonese channels, opening a window for audiences in South China on life among the capitalists. Learn Cantonese quickly if your ambition includes merging into the local popular culture, for much can be gleaned through these programmes – including local colloquialisms, and people's attitudes, concerns and priorities.

Cinema and Video

Hong Kong's film industry has come a long way from the days of Bruce Lee and *kungfu*, but whether this progress has a positive influence on the audience is a matter of opinion; authorities blame certain types of film for glamorizing criminal elements in our society. Hong Kong films enjoy world-wide circulation, although most of them are made for Cantonese-speaking audiences. Once in a while, there is a blockbuster like *Ninja Turtles* or a sensitive production like *Iron and Silk*. Nine times out of ten, however, Hong Kong films are not made for Western taste or humour.

At the end of 1993 there were 190 cinema theatres in Hong Kong. The new cinemas are comfortable and have satisfactory acoustics – a great improvement. Seats are pre-assigned. It is also nice to have smoking and eating banned. All films are censored. In 1993, 1,399 films were submitted to the censorship board for classification. Films are classified into one of three categories: #1, suitable for all ages; #2, not suitable for children; and #3, suitable only for adults over 18. Even so, the censors wield their scissors freely. If you are partial to sex and violence on the screen there is no need to feel cheated, however, for a great deal of steam and blood remain. Once in a long while, a film is withdrawn because the Xinhua News Agency objects to its political content.

Cinema sound is turned up sufficiently to waken the dead. So, if you are hard of hearing, do not let that keep you from going to the movies. Whatever the language on the sound track, subtitles are provided. If the dialogue is in Cantonese or Putonghua, English and Chinese subtitles appear. If the dialogue is in English, the subtitles are in Chinese. If you find the subtitles distracting, you will soon learn to ignore them.

If you do not enjoy going to the cinema, and find all television programmes abominable, there is no need to worry. Video rental/ purchase is a big business in Hong Kong, and video shops can be found in every neighbourhood and almost every shopping centre. Plunk down a sum of money, and membership is yours. If you are too busy to go to the shops in person, transactions can be conducted over the telephone; you will hear an efficient and pleasant voice, and the video tape or laser disc will be delivered to your home at an appointed time. Take-out food, be it simply beer and pizza or a more elaborate repast, also can be ordered by fax or telephone. This kind of service is still an affordable luxury in Hong Kong.

Copyright Laws and Piracy

If piracy of the printed word is not a major concern in Hong Kong, it is perhaps because relatively little money is involved. Compared with popular music tapes, video tapes, computer software and TV games, infringement of somebody else's copyright is insignificant. The Customs and Excise Department agents, the Government's ears and eyes for these transgressions, raid local manufacturers and retail shops from time to time. As these efforts are sporadic, the pirates return with predictable frequency. Triad-controlled gang members, some as young as thirteen, hawk pirated disks of Cantopop recordings on the streets in popular shopping areas, protected by equally youthful Triad members. Before you consign these selfish oafs to an under-world reserved for thieves and robbers, for profiteering on other people's intellectual property, imagine how many people you know actually pay for the software programmes in their computers.

TRANSPORT

For a mostly privately owned but Government franchised system, Hong Kong's public transport works well. There is an exciting amount of variety, and the prices are right. Although some aspects of the service could be much improved, venturesome visitors – and residents like you – sensibly sample all of them. You must try the new escalator, from Central to Mid-Levels. At 800 metres, with a climb of 135 metres, it is the longest in the world. It goes down towards town until ten in the morning, after which it does what its name implies.

The Ferries

Hong Kong, after all, is a watery world – joined together by its ferries. They cross Victoria Harbour, between various points on Hong Kong Island, Kowloon, and the New Territories; and they thread through the South China Sea to the outlying islands. Whether or not you always cross the harbour by the Star Ferry, you must try taking a boat

The Star Ferry, in which a First Class crossing between Kowloon and Hong Kong Island is affordable – still.

to more than one outlying island. Even in the First Class, a ferry ride provides an interesting sociological study of the Hong Kong populace. Ferries that carry vehicles are alas no longer in service; but have no fear, others continue to carry passengers everywhere. In one way or another, you may find a place to walk, eat and drink at weekends that will seem not a thousand miles but a hundred years from Central.

For travelling to more distant places such as Macau and ports of South China, jet-foil hover ferries are safe, fast and relatively free of hassle; their speed will not reduce your enjoyment of the scenery *en route*. Legend has it that aircraft jet engines require little adaptation before they propel hydrofoils across the Pearl River's estuary. On the longer routes there are conventional steamships. You can travel on deck, or sleep the night in your own cabin.

The MTR and LRT

To the Hong Kong travelling public, long used to being snarled in traffic jams, the rapid journeys provided by the Mass Transit Railway – underground – and the Light Rail Transit – on the surface – are akin to the miraculous. Starting in 1979, the public took a while to get used to the idea of this kind of transport. Once accustomed, they took to it with enthusiasm. By the end of 1993, 2.13 million passengers were travelling on the MTR daily, with almost 300,000 commuting on the shorter LRT. The trains are modern, air-conditioned, convenient, efficient and clean – because eating, drinking and smoking are banned. Mobile telephones and pagers do not work underground, so the trains are also comparatively quiet. The MTR connects with the light railway, which has stops in the New Territories all the way to the Chinese border.

Trams and the Peak Tram

Electricity-powered trams have run on street tracks across the north of the Island since 1904. Today, Hong Kong Tramway Limited operates 163 double-decked cars: east-west, parallel to the coastline.

Tram traffic on Hong Kong Island.

In 1993 they carried 340,000 passengers daily. (You may hire one of the specially decorated trams, through the Hong Kong Tourist Association, as a novel setting for a private party. The tram will go along the tracks from its western terminus to the end of the line, finishing in a fruit and vegetable market.) For ordinary commuting, it is direct and on street level so, if you do not mind crowded travel at a snail's pace, you will enjoy the tram ride. Get onto the tram at the back, work your way forward to pay your fare, and further forward to alight. You will have the unique sensation of being in the middle of the street, yet safe from the moving traffic. You can see the shops on both sides of the street, as well as all the pedestrians rushing from place to place. The top deck offers the more interesting experience but, if you are over five feet eight inches tall, you will not be able to walk (or stand) upright.

The Peak Tram is a funicular railway, hauled by cable from the lower end of Garden Road to Victoria Peak. At first privately owned, with the Kadoories as the largest shareholders, the Peak Tram is now controlled by the Hong Kong and Shanghai Hotels. The Peak Tram's construction accelerated development of the Peak as a residential area. It climbs 373 metres on gradients as steep as 45 degrees. The cars are parallel to the flat ground so, as you rise or descend, you see buildings at an angle. The best place to sit is on the right side of the car to the rear as you ascend. When you descend, you will be sitting backwards; but there is no cause for fear. The Peak Tram has been in operation since 1888 without a single accident – despite the antics of young expatriate boys of bygone years climbing onto the back of the cars while they were moving. The line serves 9,000 passengers daily – tourists and residents.

The Peak Tram noses its way up to a panoramic view of Hong Kong Harbour.

Double-deckers and Minibuses

On a less elevated plane but still above ground, the Hong Kong public travels on rubber tyres in buses and minibuses. The 386,904 motor vehicles registered in 1991 included all but the tramcars.

Of the four and a half thousand public buses in Hong Kong, over four thousand are double-deckers. Buses carry 3.4 million passengers a day. Originally blue or red and bought from Leyland Motors of Yorkshire, manufacturers of London Transport double-deckers, the Hong Kong fleets now include German and Japanese vehicles. Many of the buses have burst out in bright hues with advertisements on their exteriors.

Bus stops are places to test the Darwinian theory of survival of the fittest. At older bus stops, metal barriers have been placed to ensure order, but at the newer Citybus stops, it is still every woman for herself. We may further test our agility by trying to climb to the upper deck as the bus pitches and yaws through Hong Kong's steep and narrow roads.

Not all the roads are suitable for the double- or even single-deckers; hence the minibus, seating either 16 or 18 passengers. There are two species of minibus: with green stripes or red, on a basic beige. The red striped minibuses are for private hire, while the green follow their pre-determined routes. The destination of each green minibus is displayed above the windscreen, as is the fare. The style is friendly and informal, but the standard of cleanliness varies. When you discover the minibus route you want to use, it won't be long before you catch onto the routine. You wave at the driver to stop. Just before you want to get off, you yell 'stop'; or the same command in Cantonese, sounding like '*look chair*' but without the *k* and the *r*. It would be nice if you added a 'please' but, whatever sounds you utter, the driver will know that you want to get off. When you alight say 'thank you' to the driver in any language, especially if you are a regular rider. The gesture will be greatly appreciated – since his is a pretty boring life, and an exacting one, manoeuvring a bus through thick traffic day in and day out – and, eventually, he will remember you so that he can then be relied upon not to shut the door until both your feet are on the street. There were 6,904 minibuses in Hong Kong in 1993. The green-striped Public Light Buses carry 728,000 passengers daily, while the red-striped Private Light Buses carry 1,007,000 commuters.

Taxis

Next to various issues involving Filipina domestics, the favourite topic on *Letters to the Editor* pages of Hong Kong's English-language newspapers seems to be complaints about taxi drivers. It is true that the demand for taxis far exceeds the supply. Taxis in the New Territories, numbering 2,738 by 1993 reckoning, are painted bright green, and the 14,950 in Kowloon and Hong Kong Island are painted dark crimson. Licence fees are high, and the number of licences issued is limited. It is not true that taxi ownership is controlled by a syndicate. Many cabs are owned by individual drivers, who drive the cabs themselves during the day shift of seven to five, then lease the taxis to other drivers for the night shift. If the night drivers seem carefree, paying scant attention to speed limit or markings on the road, it is because they are younger than the day-time drivers to begin with, and are on their second job.

Fare increases require Government consent. The taxis are metered, and it is extremely difficult to cheat on the meter. At one time writers to *The Editor* expressed their concern about the compact size of the newer taxis, claiming that smaller wheels covered shorter distances each revolution, thereby making journeys more expensive – because the meters clicked on in proportion to the speed at which the wheels went round. Then a new topic of complaint emerged, about drivers taking circuitous routes to increase the length of the ride. Complaints became concentrated on taxi drivers' preference for the Eastern Corridor and the New Tunnel to the airport, for instance, adding another 30 dollars to the fare. In actuality, when the Cross Harbour Tunnel is congested, going by the New Tunnel can cut the journey from Central to Kaitak by almost twenty minutes, though it is more expensive.

It used to be a dirty towel, but now it is a red card, displayed on the windscreen to show that the taxi is off duty. This act is illegal, but the law is rarely enforced. The drivers do go off duty, and the change of shifts takes place between three-thirty and five. Kowloon taxis in

Hong Kong and Hong Kong taxis in Kowloon like to put up the 'Out of service' sign, so that they need not respond to signals of passengers not going their way. Probably they would not know how to find your destination anyhow, if they happened to be caught on the wrong side of the harbour. When you have been here for a while, you will know where best to catch a taxi going your way. With the MTR and buses using tunnels, fewer people are taking taxis, but cabs are still hard to find during rush hours and on rainy days.

As in all major cities, when it rains in Hong Kong available taxis disappear. There are taxis, but not for you. You can call all the taxi numbers in the telephone book, but nothing will come. The offer of an extra ten dollars – now going up to twenty – will bring about a miracle, but you wouldn't want to become a part of the system spreading corruption would you? Here you are, a person needing to arrive somewhere within a short span of time: are you going to be guided by your principles of fairness, or are you going to play ball with the local system and not miss your appointment or your aircraft?

Driving in Hong Kong

A Hong Kong driving licence is expensive, but there is no need for you to go in person. If you have a licence valid in your own country – one acknowledged by the Hong Kong Government as requiring all licensed drivers to know how to drive – you can send a messenger to obtain the forms to apply for a Hong Kong licence. The messenger can stand and wait until your name is called, and pick up your licence when it is ready. Unless you attend to these formalities yourself, however, you will miss the special experience of waiting for your licence at the Motor Vehicles Department – akin only to that of waiting for your identity card to be processed or your residence visa to be issued at the Hong Kong Immigration Department. There are 1,008,270 licensed drivers in the territory; and 'moving violations' can disqualify you from driving.

If you think that our roads are crowded, you have the Governor's figures to support your contention. There are 270 motor vehicles per kilometre of Hong Kong's roads. Every car seems to be on the road at the same time and in much the same place as yours. Being native here, the drivers want to take advantage of every minute and of every inch of space. Therefore, as you politely wait in a long queue trying alternately to merge into one or another tunnel lane, other drivers will push ahead of you from all directions. While you remember the admonitions of your driving teacher to keep a safe distance from the car in front, do not be surprised if some other car cuts right in between. It is like getting into an office lift: you must be on your guard lest you lose your space.

Take the traffic regulations very, very seriously. They are strictly enforced at all times.

By Boat, Plane, Train, Bus, Car and Subway to China

The number of people in Hong Kong is not decreasing. Immigrants continue to arrive from China. In 1993 alone, 52.5 million passengers travelled between China and Hong Kong. You can fly from here to all the major cities, and to a number of smaller cities that are not a part of the general vocabulary, such as Changchun in Manchuria or Chengdu in Sichuan; but plane reservations are difficult to obtain. It is possible to go by ferry or hovercraft to ports of the Guangdong province, or by water to Macau and cross the border there. The non-stop train to Guangzhou is easy and comfortable; and, if you want adventure, you can take the train, with changes of course, all the way from Hong Kong to London, via the Trans-Siberian Railway. Buses are now running between Hong Kong and nearby points to the north; some will take you to more than passable golf courses in the morning, and bring you home that very evening. With the appropriate licences, you are even allowed to drive into China by car.

The most unbelievable and least expensive way to travel to China – and most of the Hong Kong populace 'commute' in this way – is by MTR, and then transfer to a local train of the Canton-Kowloon

Railway as far as Lowu; from there one walks across the border to China. During a holiday weekend, more than half a million enterprising souls will cross and return in this way.

Regardless of the route, you still need to obtain a visa to visit China. If your business requires you to make frequent trips, a multiple-entry visa is issued by the Chinese visa office here for six months at a time. Otherwise, single or two-trip visas can be had on the spot.

Patience and perseverance are the key words in making your travel arrangements to China. Unless you plan long in advance, you will be lucky if you can get a seat on a plane during the busy months of spring, summer and autumn. An acquaintance of ours decided on a Saturday that he needed to be in Beijing on Monday afternoon. His office and his spouse worked with two sets of travel agents to secure him a seat on any flight to Beijing on Saturday, Sunday or Monday; and finally obtained a confirmed seat on a Monday flight that would have him in Beijing at supper time, too late for his appointment. So, on Sunday morning, he arrived at Kaitak a little after eleven and began to stand in the queue of the airline that promised him the possibility of a seat on one of its flights to Beijing. He was number 62 on the list of passengers waiting for a seat. Finally he managed to fly to Beijing on the 7:14 pm flight, First Class.

Do not expect polite and efficient service from the ground personnel. These young men and women are so hassled that they behave as if they were doing you a big favour by checking you in at all. Their command of English – and Cantonese, come to that – has deteriorated so much that, since they are tired and are not willing to listen, you feel that you should be grateful if they issue you a boarding pass for the correct flight. Any special request is greeted with sullen silence, if not rude mumbling. They could not care less whether you lose or keep your temper.

Air Travel to Everywhere
Kaitak is a modern airport but, situated as it is in the middle of the city,

the night hours are deemed unsuitable for planes lest excessive noise disturb the residents. Apart from the Macau ferries and boats and trains from South China, and the occasional cruise ship, travellers arrive at and leave Hong Kong by air. Major international as well as regional and Asian national airlines stop at Kaitak, carrying passengers and cargo to everywhere in the world. Hong Kong's own Cathay Pacific is prominent among them. Currently, 24.5 million passengers a year come and go on slightly fewer than 300 flights scheduled daily between 8:30 in the morning and midnight. In 1993, 1.14 million tonnes of cargo passed through Kaitak.

The Hong Kong Government is expending much energy and resources in the development and promotion of a new airport at Chek Lap Kok, just north of Lantau Island, planned to be opened in 1997. This is an enormous project, involving reclamation of land and the construction of railways, roads and bridges, besides commercial and industrial developments. The financing of the project will need to carry beyond 30 June 1997, so the Chinese Government demands a

An artist's impression of the new airport at Chek Lap Kok, Lantau Island.

voice in decisions that will affect future obligations of the Hong Kong Special Administrative Zone.

The new airport has been – or has provided – a major area of disagreement between the Chinese and the Hong Kong Governments since 1990.

CONCLUSION

This discussion of infrastructure and facilities has not included specialised interests such as port development. Nevertheless it shows that Hong Kong is very much a metropolitan city of the modern world.

Chapter Six

WORK AND LEISURE

In the final analysis, regardless of personal prejudices, work comes first in Hong Kong. For those with leisure time, playing is important too. Keep in mind, however, that there is very little social entertaining in the pure sense. The adage that there is no such thing as a free lunch is perhaps more true in Hong Kong than anywhere else.

THE OFFICE HIERARCHY

Whatever the nature or size of your business, please remember that the office structure in Hong Kong, like its society, is hierarchical. Whereas a clear line of authority is good management policy in the West, it is essential in the Hong Kong culture. Any blurring of the line will lead to confusion and resentment sooner or later. The office hierarchy is determined by position, but age and gender of the employees also come into consideration. The business aspects of the hierarchy are easy to handle because divisions and layers of line and staff functions can be defined. It is the other aspects of office life that are more difficult to delineate. It is easier if you have a small office, because most likely the staff will be sharing various aspects of the routine of the office in addition to their specifically assigned work – following your example, one hopes – but, if you have more than four or five staff in your office, pay attention to the hierarchy even if you are democratic by inclination.

Do not blur this line. Hong Kong office workers have a keen sense of which tasks are more menial than others and therefore beneath their dignified station in the hierarchy. You must be careful and respect the hierarchy. You do not ask a junior clerk to give a message to the department head, especially if it can be interpreted as an order. You do not ask the secretary to go down to the post office, a job ordinarily done by messengers, or to change a light bulb, a chore always performed by a handyman. Another example: never go to the back office to make yourself a cup of coffee or tea, unless you want to give the tea lady a heart attack by sending the message that you are getting ready to dismiss her. Problems of this nature are solving themselves, though, as tea ladies are a disappearing breed; while those that remain are getting so used to the antics of a group of younger expats in trying to do everything themselves, that they are no longer so easily upset by a single annoying act.

When in doubt, use your common sense and pass all your orders down the line through your secretary and the department heads. They will know what to do to preserve everyone's dignity and your composure.

There are sub-cultures in the office hierarchy, noticeable by their dress. The lower the rank, the more assiduously the women follow the latest Hong Kong fashion and the men adopt the mannerisms of the latest Cantopop star. You can always spot a messenger – male or female – by the not-too-loose blue jeans and running shoes, with a Walkman attached to the waist and ear. Uniforms which shop assistants and bank tellers sport with pride are not a part of the job identification desired by office messengers. Do not offend the messengers, for they are the most difficult employees to hire. Their turnover is high, and advertisements for them often go unanswered.

THE JOB DESCRIPTION

Titles and job description are important to staff because they derive a sense of security from having their duties defined in black and white. The titles show the line of authority. The job descriptions tell each employee what his or her duties are supposed to be.

Until and unless a rapport is established, and sometimes not even then, staff will not perform any chore which they perceive to be below their status and which is not specified in their job descriptions. They will not tell you that the chore is not a part of their job, for they know that talking back to the boss is rude, and speaking one's mind openly is not a characteristic of the Hong Kong culture. They will grumble behind your back, sometimes within your hearing, but definitely not to your face. Moreover, they will ignore your request. Now you know why you hire a telephone-cleaning service: because nobody can decide whose job it is to perform the menial task of keeping the telephones clean. You also hire a cleaning crew to empty the waste-paper baskets, but shredding confidential documents at the end of the day is not considered a demeaning task.

OFFICE ETIQUETTE

Even if you work in a casual style and generally run the business in a low-keyed way, staff see the gap between you and them as being important. You can be pleasant and say 'good morning', 'please' and 'thank you'; and praise workers for a job well done. Criticism, on the other hand, should be delivered gently, and it is more effective if sent through the proper channel. It is essential to keep your dignity, and a certain distance from your staff. It is fine to be friendly, but over-familiarity makes it difficult to maintain command in the Hong Kong culture.

Office workers today come from a wider background than they did a dozen or so years ago. With the reduction in factory jobs, and an increasing demand for workers in offices and in service industries, young men and women who otherwise would have been bent over machines are now working in offices, restaurants, airline counters or hotels – where they have to relate to people in a variety of unpredictable situations. These young men and women come from homes where all decisions are made by their parents. They buy lunch boxes to eat at their desks, and so lose their best chance for developing social skills. Very likely their social circle is confined to families and relatives. They live in housing estates, and return there to spend all their non-working hours. The expats in the office are probably the only non-Cantonese people they meet.

They know their places and, while working hard at their jobs and eager to please, they are reluctant to venture beyond the responsibilities specified in their job descriptions. They are inarticulate, they cannot cope with what they perceive to be insults or unjustified criticisms, and they sulk. Or they resign without telling you or their direct supervisor what is bothering them. When a staff member leaves because he is going 'for further studies in Canada', you should know that either he has found a better paying job with another firm, or he has resented something said or done to him.

Staff members do not have an over-view of what you are trying to accomplish. Spending from 9:00 to 5:00 or 8:30 to 6:00 five days a week, with half an hour for lunch, and from 9:00 to 12:30 or 1:00 on Saturdays, concentrating on their narrow tasks, cannot be unmitigated fascination all the time. Do not expect any flexibility. Call it the failure of the Hong Kong education system if you will, but workers have not been trained to make decisions or to use their judgement.

Some of them may be extremely proficient at operating the computer but they cannot read a manual, nor are they willing to learn anything new by themselves. If you tell them to take the manual home to study so that they can improve their knowledge, they are reluctant. They do not say no, they just do not take the manual home. Self-training from the manual during their time away from the office is not a part of the job description. Besides, the conditions at home may not permit quiet study. If you want them to learn anything new, they would like to attend a training course at your expense and during office hours. At the end of the training course, there is a certificate, which is important for the employee's curriculum vitae – and future work.

While they stay with you, however, the staff are conscientious and work very hard. Productivity in Hong Kong is high. They are serious, well groomed, and cheerful. Perhaps they prefer a male boss to a female one, and take instructions better from men; but, in general, Hong Kong women are good administrators because they are good with details. Try not to lose your cool or raise your voice. You will scare the staff. They will leave you 'for further studies in Canada' and you will have to hire and train replacements.

Part of the perks of working in an office is the bubbly soda provided by you. The staff drink soda because they like its sweet taste, and because it is worth money. Consumption of one or two tins a day means that you spend on their behalf another fifteen to twenty dollars a week – tantamount to a rise in pay. A young Chinese-American woman we know worked for the representative office of an American bank here one summer when she was a college student. She was asked why she did not drink soda in the office, especially at nine o'clock in the morning. 'You can drink tea at home,' advised her Hong Kong Chinese colleague, 'and soda is expensive.' If you tell the staff that soda is not good for their teeth you only reinforce their conviction that *gweilos* are miserly. Chuck the cost to office expenses and be happy in the satisfaction that this is a cheap way to buy goodwill.

Fireworks on the second night of the Lunar New Year. You would not want to miss this extravaganza, for you won't see a better firework show anywhere in the world.

Start Work Laisee

Another red packet of *laisee* is to be given to each employee by the boss on the first day after the Lunar New Year holidays. This one is called the *Start Work Laisee*. The big boss gives the *laisee* to everybody in the office, while you, if you are small fry, give it only to people under your immediate command. Do not overstep the boundary. Remember the office hierarchy. It is not obligatory to give this packet, but giving it brings you yet again a great deal of goodwill and makes a cheerful beginning to another year of working together. The Hong Kong Chinese term for working together is 'we co-operate'. The amount in each packet does not need to be large. We know people who buy a HK$25 MTR stored-value ticket for each employee; also bosses who put in a two dollar coin. The employees will be happier if they know that the gesture has come from you personally, and is not just more largesse from the company.

The First Name Syndrome

Employees in Hong Kong are becoming lax, and a worker with good manners is increasingly difficult to find. For instance, strangers half your age are calling you by your first name. Few people in Hong Kong like this informality, and almost everybody is denouncing the Americans for bringing their casual style of mixing business and personal relationships. The Americans are certainly more democratic and do tend to treat everybody as equals, but you cannot put the blame on the Americans for the first name syndrome in Hong Kong. People in New York and Washington may address you over the telephone as 'honey', but they are still likely to call you by your surname preceded by a proper title.

Nor, probably, does much of the blame stem from each culture seeing the other as putting the last name first.

When a sales person representing your company telephones a prospective client to solicit business, calling the client by his or her first name is discourteous. It is adding further insult to injury when the salesman introduces himself as *Mister* Da. No client is going to react favourably when your salesman says over the telephone: 'Is this Mary? I am calling about renew the service contract in your Macintosh computer (sic). My name is Mister Da of XYZ Company.'

Sales people are not the only offenders in Hong Kong today. Travel agents and secretaries have also taken to calling people they have not met by their first names. Perhaps they hear you calling your business associates by their first names and are following suit. Perhaps you allow them to call you by your first name, or you may even think that you are improving the office culture by having staff address the bosses by their first names. Whatever makes you comfortable is perfectly all right, because you must have your own style in running your office. Do remember, however, that the Hong Kong culture is much more formal. Do let your staff call you Bob if it makes you feel more comfortable, but make sure that they address your clients, whether in person or over the telephone, as Mr Wong or

135

Mrs Chen, not David or Shirley. If your surname is unpronounceable, perhaps Tchaikovsky or even Ronan, have them call you Mr John, or Mr Bill, or Miss Katharine or whatever, but do make sure that your secretary refers to you as Mr Tchaikovsky to people outside and inside your office. Over-friendliness leads to sloppy business relationships. In the case of Mary and the Macintosh computer, she did not renew her service contract, despite repeated telephoning from Mr Da, a Miss Lo, and a Ms Bo – all addressing her as Mary.

The Executive Secretary

Good secretaries are a rare species; one may be the best friend you will ever have in Hong Kong. Since you are an executive, she likes to sport the title Executive Secretary. It is only fitting because she manages your business and social calendar, arranges your travel, interfaces between you and the rest of your office, and guards you against the outside world. She makes sure that your correspondence looks beautiful, and that all your files are organized. She also helps you and your family in a myriad ways because you know neither Cantonese nor the local way of getting things accomplished. She is loyal and protective: in time, she will anticipate your moods and put up with your idiosyncrasies. Above all, she pampers rather than challenges your ego.

Secretaries in Hong Kong are receiving higher salaries than they did a decade ago, but their earnings are still far below those of your other associates. Your secretary will make your tea or coffee or, rather, instruct people in the back office to make it for you. She will not mind running personal errands for you and your spouse, but would hate to be asked to shop for birthday presents for members of your family. What a secretary most dislikes is having to tell lies to cover for the boss when the boss is, for reasons for his own, unwilling to confront the caller himself. Experienced good secretaries are hard to find. When executives change jobs in Hong Kong, they usually take their secretaries with them.

The Etiquette of the Name Card

Calling (or business) cards are known as name cards in Hong Kong. It is a direct translation from the Chinese *min* (name) and *pian* (small card). The term that means *name on a small card* is actually more fitting than *calling card*, because these cards are not used to call on people any more, but in introducing to you a person you are meeting for the first time, and you to the person who is meeting you. Your card should have your name, title, the name and address of your company, and your office telephone and fax numbers. In Hong Kong, the card also sports the logo of your company, for a logo is perceived as something inseparable from a worthwhile company.

An employee who represents your company to outsiders should have name cards. A name card identifies him as a member of the company, acknowledging that the company is proud of the association. It also gives his correct name and where people can find him. Always carry a supply of cards with you when you venture out of the office. If a person you meet gives you his name card and you do not offer one in return, it signals to him either that you do not wish to make his acquaintance, or that you have no status at all. Remember, a person with no label in Hong Kong is without legitimacy.

Your Name in Chinese

Expatriates in Hong Kong like to have their names rendered in Chinese. Your colleagues will do this for you, transliterating your surname into Cantonese. Probably there is already a Chinese surname which may fit yours nicely, and Hong Kong Chinese are wonderfully clever in finding appropriate characters to suit the sounds of your name. All the characters they find for you will have lucky implications. However, if you do not want the ordinary Chinese renditions of more common first names, such as John into Yo-han (which may sound like a well-known Japanese department store), ask one of your more literary friends to organize a name for you. Avoid companies which transliterate names for a fee. They have no sense of humour and little literary heritage.

137

It is even more important that your Chinese name should sound acceptable in Putonghua. Whereas Hong Kong people will know you by your name in its original language or its English version – because everybody you meet will understand at least some English – in mainland China or Taiwan you will certainly be recognized only by your Chinese name. You will not want your name in Putonghua to sound rude or like something the cat might have dragged in. So, think hard and choose wisely; do not take the first name given to you. Consult everybody you know who understands Cantonese or Putonghua. As a Sinologist, Lord Wilson possessed a Chinese name long before he was appointed Governor of Hong Kong in 1987. His surname in Chinese was Wei, a character with three radicals which could also stand separately. Two of the radicals, as it turned out, were unacceptable to the Hong Kong Chinese because by themselves they were the characters for *woman* and *ghost*. Lord Wilson had to select another character among the more than fifty with the Wei sound.

Office Christmas Cards

It is becoming a fad for companies to send Christmas as well as Lunar New Year cards to all business friends and associates. Use your own judgement whether you wish to join this merry throng. Find out the practice of your predecessors and listen to what your colleagues think you ought to do. A number of charities sell Christmas cards to raise funds, so you will have plenty of choice. Select the cards you like for their aesthetic quality or for the charity you wish to support. Ask your office manager to handle the card details or, if you do not have an office manager, ask your secretary. If you want to combine your office and personal lists, consult your spouse. The Post Office publishes date and weight information for overseas Christmas mail. To avoid squandering your or your firm's earnings on airmail you might manage a mass mailing in October. It might then suit the Post Office to send this surface mail by air at its expense. You may then be surprised by a flurry of heavily stamped return cards early in November.

DUTIES, TAXES AND SUNDRY FEES

Despite Hong Kong's reputation as a free port, there are duties on the 'import, export, manufacture, sale and storage' of various classes of goods, notably alcoholic beverages and tobacco. There are direct taxes on personal and corporate income: salaries tax on individual earnings and profit tax on company returns. Though it may come as a surprise to Americans under the illusion that stamp duties had disappeared as a result of the American Revolution, let us assure you that they thrive in Hong Kong. Revenue is derived from stamps on all taxed transactions, including share transfers. Rates, property tax, a gambling tax on racing bets and lottery proceeds, death duties on estates of over 5 million dollars, a tariff on hotel rooms and entertainment, and charges on Government-operated utilities and services, including the airport tax, vehicle registrations and driving licences – all contribute substantially to the exchequer. A big windfall for the Government comes now and then from the sale of land, much of it more than repaying the cost of reclamation from the sea. All this explains why Hong Kong has a balanced budget with a mammoth Surplus Reserve Fund.

Do not run foul of the Inland Revenue Department. There is an assessment section and another section known as collection. Your salaries tax is assessed at the end of your first year of employment here by the Assessment Section. Then the Collections Section will send a notice for you to pay the taxes for two years – the year past and the year to come. The two sections do not appear to speak to each other. Once any of their computers has you on its files, you and its version of your details are there forever, regardless of what human voices might say. The amount overpaid (including the consequences of any overestimate) will be returned to you when you leave Hong Kong. In any case, remember that patience is a virtue.

MONEY

Money is important in all modern cultures, and Hong Kong's is no exception. This is a wonderful town if you have plenty of money, principally because whatever goods and services money can buy are available here. Money is taken very seriously by everybody. If to you some people seem to have gone a little wild in the pursuit and spending of money, it is because only during the past decade or so have they been able to share in the prosperity of Hong Kong. Until then, spendable cash was the preserve of a few; today, almost everyone has a chance to earn some. Every other word out of people's mouths seems to be *chien* or *qian*, money; but not everyone lacks a sense of balance on this subject. There are people who give generously to help society's less fortunate. Lavish entertainment, however, is never without reason, if only to show other people that you are successful; for, in Hong Kong, success is measured in terms of money.

As 1997 nears, there is a sense of urgency on the part of some people to build up a nest egg, so the accumulation of money seems to have become an end in itself. Headlines about illegal and unethical acquisition of money are made from time to time; but tradesmen who cut a corner or two, by cheating their customers, to earn the extra dollar or two are no longer considered newsworthy. Big time crooks who take Hong Kong for billions, including once-respected bankers and financiers, are still making the front page years after the demise of their schemes. Sexual exploitation, and robbery of banks and jewellers, have always been integral to the Hong Kong scene; but in general the people work hard and honestly for their money. Meanwhile, they know that money does fall from the sky; and are certain that it is only a matter of time before their turn comes. Hence, they gamble. The term *fat choy* is a standard greeting, by no means limited to the Lunar New Year season.

Banking and High Finance
At the end of 1993, there were 172 licensed banks, representative offices of 142 foreign banks, and several dozen of the investment and

merchant banks known by statute as 'restricted licence' banks. Thirty of the banks are locally incorporated, with almost 1,605 branches spread through the territory. What you will want to know is where you can deposit your money and muster enough cash for a long weekend. There is no need to fret. There is an ATM machine around every corner and in all shopping malls. Credit cards are accepted everywhere.

The Hongkong and Shanghai Banking Corporation and the Standard Chartered Bank issue Hong Kong currency. In 1994, the Bank of China became the third issuing bank in Hong Kong.

The Stock Market

Any figures given here for the Hong Kong Stock Exchange will be out of date when you read this book, because buying and selling activity is so volatile. Since the scandal involving the founder and top officials of the Exchange during the early 1980s, its activities have been closely monitored by the autonomous Securities and Futures Commission, set up in 1989. At the end of 1992, the Exchange had 620 corporate and individual members. In 1993, sixty-eight newly listed companies were added to the market; six of these are state-owned enterprises of the People's Republic of China. Only members may trade on the Exchange. The Hang Seng Index was at 5,512, with an average daily turnover of 2.8 billion dollars, as 1992 ended. The average daily turnover in 1991 was $1.3 billion, rising to $2.8 in 1992 and $4.9 in 1993.

These advances in share prices were nothing compared with what was to come in late 1993. Out of the blue, it seems, the world discovered Hong Kong shares as a way into future growth in East Asia generally and China in particular. After North American money poured into Hong Kong shares on Friday 29 October, 1993, the Hang Seng Index rose 318 points from the day before, to 8,389. On that day 2,789,074,806 shares changed hands, valued at HK$9,723,042,278. After the two-day weekend hiatus, the Hang Seng Index leaped another 300 or so points on Monday, 1 November, a rise of 3.22 per cent, to close at 9,629 – money having poured in from Japan, North America and Hong Kong itself. The Exchange, totally computerized, coped with aplomb. It emerged with colours flying. Six months later the Index had *recovered* to that level.

GIVE US HONG KONG'S DAILY BREAD

The rice-eating people of Hong Kong consume 920 tonnes of the grain every day. That is to say about two million pounds of rice go down the Hong Kong hatch seven times a week: an impressive record indeed. Although all of the rice is imported – principally from China, Thailand, and Australia – Hong Kong produces some of the other foods for its people. They devour daily 1,020 tonnes of vegetables, 1,060 pigs, 410 head of cattle, 280 tonnes of poultry (chickens, ducks, geese, pigeons and quail), 550 tonnes of fish and 1,460 tonnes of fruit. An estimated 480,000 litres of milk (42 per cent locally produced and fresh) is consumed, some of it in baking. Local production accounts for 26 per cent of the vegetables, 27 per cent of live poultry, 6 per cent of the pigs, 12 per cent of freshwater fish (cultivated in fish farms) and 63 per cent of total fish consumption. Actually, the local production of vegetables and livestock has declined, because stringent health and pollution control keeps below-standard farmers from selling their produce, and because farmland has been developed into housing estates.

Every kind of foodstuff is imported fresh, preserved or frozen from all areas of the world. Animals imported live are slaughtered here, those imported direct to the abattoirs not needing to go into quarantine. China and Taiwan are the leading suppliers of Hong Kong's imported foodstuffs, followed by the United States, Korea, Singapore, Germany and the United Kingdom. While the Hong Kong Chinese will take fresh meat from the butchers, they insist on seeing seafood and poultry live before paying for them. (Somehow, the local public believes that Western foods come only in tins – hence the popularity of such foods as tinned sardines and chopped ham.) They take for granted that an international array of foods should appear regularly on the shelves of ordinary supermarkets. You, on the other hand, will find what is available at the supermarkets and delicatessens truly sensational. It is like going to Bloomingdales in New York or Harrods in London.

MANUFACTURING

After the mid-1980s, manufacturing in Hong Kong declined. Increased labour costs and high rents led manufacturers to move their production facilities to other Asian countries and especially China. Joint venture factories were set up in Shanghai, Guangdong and Fujian. In 1984, 41.7 percent of all employees in Hong Kong (904,709) worked in the manufacturing sector. In 1992, only 23.3 per cent (571,181), worked in 41,937 factories – to make clothing, textiles, electronics, watches, clocks, plastics and toys. Once the garment manufacturing capital of the world, Hong Kong makes only designer clothing today.

Hong Kong's manufacturers are not hampered by labour unrest. Although there are several federations of industrial workers, the labour union movement is neither militant nor strike-oriented. The unions' concerns have been in the area of industrial safety.

TRADE

Hong Kong is one of the ten leaders, by volume and value, in international trade. Its major trading partners are China, the United States and Japan. Being the principal entrepôt for China's trade with the rest of the world, Hong Kong and its businessmen are intensely interested in China maintaining its Most Favoured Nation status with the United States. The value of imports and exports in 1993 was 2,118,851 million Hong Kong dollars, with 1,072,597 million in imports and 223,027 million in domestic exports plus 823, 227 in re-exports.

A multi-talented and entrepreneurial artisan at work. He offers spectacles and curios as well as scrolls of painting and calligraphy.

Hong Kong's manufacturers depend on imported raw materials. These items include iron and steel, woven cotton fabrics and artificial fibres, raw materials for plastics, watch and clock movements, and textile machinery. In 1992, 41 per cent of imports were in this category. They included clothing, radios, television sets, stereo and tape-recorder equipment, records and discs, shoes, toys, games and sporting goods, plus luggage and travel equipment. With the rise in value of the *yen*, consumer goods imported from Japan are becoming extremely expensive for the residents. They are no longer bargains for tourists either.

In retail trade, besides the shopping malls, department stores and specialist boutiques, there are neighbourhood stores selling perhaps a pint – sorry, half a litre – of milk at a time, or a small loaf of bread, or a stack of red *laisee* packets and some letter writing paper. They are known as the *si-dou*, a Cantonese rendering of the English word *store*. There is one in your neighbourhood, no matter where you live – unless high rents have driven it away recently. While other shops close around dinner time, the *si-dou* is open seven days a week from the crack of dawn until long after dinner.

HOSPITALS AND HEALTH CARE

The Government operates a good system of hospitals and clinics, which provides sound health care at very low cost. The University of Hong Kong and the Chinese University of Hong Kong both have medical schools, and their personnel staff the Queen Mary Hospital and the Prince of Wales Hospital. Waiting lists for non-emergency services are long, and facilities are overcrowded. Since 1991, the newly established Hospital Authority has assumed responsibility for the management and control of Government hospitals. There are also private hospitals and clinics in Hong Kong, each with its own following. British residents appear to prefer the Matilda Hospital on the Peak, while Americans and Japanese patronize the Hong Kong Adventist Hospital – which runs an active outpatient clinic. The

Chinese prefer the Hong Kong Sanatorium because it is comfortable and home-like. The Canossian Hospital is known for its orthopaedic care. The Ruttonjee Sanatorium, which had been used for tuberculosis patients, has been rebuilt as a hospital for thoracic and pulmonary diseases.

Partnerships of physicians and surgeons operate here as business corporations, similar to those in the United States. Individual doctors see patients in their offices. It is a universal practice of members of the medical profession not to stay on top of their appointment schedules, and Hong Kong is no exception. It is disconcerting enough to arrive at a doctor's office only to find at least three other patients sharing the time of your appointment; but when you discover the waiting room full, and the queue of patients stretching down the corridor all the way to the lift, it is time to change doctors.

Traditional Chinese Medicine

Traditional Chinese medicine is alive and thriving in Hong Kong. Chinese practitioners do not have degrees in medicine; their knowledge and skills are usually passed down from father to son, and from master to student. That is why Chinese practitioners are addressed as 'Master' instead of 'Doctor'.

The herbal masters diagnose by feeling the pulse and checking physical signs of disease with their eyes. Although medicinal herbs are still cooked over a slow fire into a bitter brew, many Chinese cures now come in capsule or pill form. Sooner or later, when you are sufficiently settled in to want to know more about Chinese traditions, you will probably walk down Queen's Road, Central, not far from Lane Crawford and the Chinese Emporium, to stop at Eu Yang Seng, a traditional Chinese medicine shop. Eu Yang Seng moved out of its old premises to make way for the escalator that goes from Central to Mid-Levels. The brightly lit new shop, directly across the street, opens onto the pavement unhampered by any wall. It has counters for selling medicines as well as display cases of herbs and other oddities

A shop selling traditional Chinese medicine.

– dried seahorse, or deer horn, for instance – with their curative values explained in Chinese and English.

Qigong is different from *tieda*; calling the practitioners of either of these schools of cure 'chiropractors' is not exactly correct. *Qigong* began as a sensible method of proper breathing and exercise and is sometimes practised alongside herbal medicine, but practitioners use their hands to massage the patient's body. It is becoming increasingly popular in Hong Kong and overseas Chinese communities. Its practitioners use a combination of massage, chiropractic, feeling of the pulse, and examination of the general colouring of the patient, to cure various diseases, including orthopaedic problems. *Tieda* practitioners, on the other hand, are rarely more than simple chiropractors and masseurs, but they also apply hot poultices of herbs to painful areas of your anatomy. The only concession they make to modernity is in enclosing the hot herbs in plastic bags so that the substance does not leak out.

147

Hong Kong is also a place for acupuncture and acupressure. Acupuncture involves needles penetrating the skin; acupressure does not. Sanitary standards have improved, but care still must be taken when you visit an acupuncture establishment. Insist on sterilized needles, for hepatitis is common in Hong Kong. Otherwise, this time-honoured way of curing pains enjoys a large and faithful following among the Chinese population, and attracts expatriates also. In general, neither traditional Chinese medicine nor its practitioners should be regarded lightly.

Veterinary Services

Hong Kong is much more caring as far as pets are concerned than you probably would have guessed, since dogs are mainly seen as utilitarian (in one way or another). Quarantine of imported animals used to last six months, but now pets are kept in for only one month. There was a time when one veterinary surgeon looked after all the animals not belonging to the Jockey Club. Today, there are veterinary clinics throughout the territory. One personable and intelligent vet, an Irishman with a delightful sense of humour and a doctorate from the University of Edinburgh, even makes house calls. Get your grapevine to tell you who he and his colleagues are, or check in the yellow pages. The Royal Society for Prevention of Cruelty to Animals is active here. The RSPCA operates the only hospital for animals in Asia. Unfortunately, as ownership of pets becomes more popular, increasing numbers of pets are abandoned; so the RSPCA has a large pound full of abandoned dogs and cats awaiting adoption.

INSTITUTIONS OF HIGHER EDUCATION

There are three universities in Hong Kong which award bachelor's, master's and doctorate degrees in the arts, humanities and sciences, and in such professions as dentistry, medicine, law, journalism, education, computer science and architecture. To meet popular demand, programmes in business administration have been added. At the University of Hong Kong, founded in 1911 and following the British system, teaching is in English except for Chinese and Chinese History Before the Modern Era. The Chinese University of Hong Kong came into being in 1963, when three colleges following the American system were amalgamated. Lectures are given in English, Cantonese or Putonghua, depending on the instructors and the students in each course. Classes began at the University of Science and Technology in 1991, with faculty composed of ethnic Chinese academics hired from North American universities. Concentrating their resources at the undergraduate level, these universities also maintain facilities for postgraduate studies and scholarly research.

Three other institutions and two polytechnic institutes are becoming empowered to award degrees. They are Lingnan College, Hong Kong Baptist College, Academy of Performing Arts, Hong Kong Polytechnic and the City Polytechnic. Operating as a school with college level courses in Hong Kong since the 1960s, Lingnan College is the heir to the pre-1949 Lingnan University of Canton. It became a degree-granting institution in 1991. Signs that its Board of Trustees is taking the College more seriously are the appointment of Professor Edward Chen, an eminent economist and public personage, as the new President, and the plans to construct a campus in the New Territories. Hong Kong Baptist College has been providing tertiary education as an alternative to the universities for decades. Academy of Performing Arts will grant its first Bachelor of Fine Arts degrees in 1995. The two polytechnics, founded to train professionals from hotel management to occupational therapy, will be granting degrees by the time you read these pages.

All of these institutions hold classes for adults in the evenings. The extra-mural classes did not begin as a part of any university curriculum, in the sense that credits accrued in this manner did not culminate in a degree. However, the evening schools have developed into something grander. The extra-mural studies department at Baptist College has grown into the School of Continuing Education, providing opportunities for Hong Kong residents to study for credits from overseas universities without leaving the territory. The extra-mural studies department of the University of Hong Kong, too, has been transformed into the School of Professional and Continuing Education.

The Open Learning Institute, which awards degrees, was established in 1989 as a distance learning tertiary institution. Students work at home, or in study centres rented by the OLI, but seldom through face-to-face teaching. Lectures or practicals on mathematics and computer studies, for instance, are televised, typically on Sunday mornings, with video copies available in the study centres. Students accumulate credits, usually at the rate of one a year, by capping each nine-month course with a three-hour examination. Six credits make a degree, perhaps in four years, perhaps in eight.

In other words, for the first time, Hong Kong people who have not been able to go to a college or university for one reason or another, immediately after finishing secondary school, may now pursue higher education even if they hold a full-time job. This is where you, as an expatriate in the community, can benefit. You may wish to work for a college degree while you are here. Or, if you already have a degree, you may want to pursue a more advanced or a more congenial one. And even if you have no degree in mind, you may take courses – interesting or useful or both – which might well include excellent language training.

THE ROYAL ASIATIC SOCIETY

Despite its somewhat cumbersome name, this Society is in Hong Kong a group of low-profile individuals whose common interest is Asia: all aspects of its peoples, arts, customs, cultures, institutions, philosophy, history, societies, traditions and so forth. Membership is open to all. It is a friendly and welcoming society with a somewhat dated name. Lectures are given by local and visiting scholars. Topics vary, but the lectures cater to an audience sharing an interest in the Continent without necessarily being specialists in any aspect of it.

Museum curators and other qualified members arrange tours to sites of cultural and historical interest in China and elsewhere. Programmes are conducted in English. The Society publishes its *Journal of the Hong Kong Branch of the Royal Asiatic Society*, supposedly once a year but with some flexibility.

MUSEUMS AND GALLERIES

The Urban Council and the universities maintain museums and galleries. Although the objects and the techniques of display are of high quality and international interest, the special focus of Hong Kong's collections is Chinese or pan-Asian. The historical museums, including The Hong Kong Museum of History and those on sites that have survived from the past, such as the Sam Tong Uk in Tsuen Wan, a restored walled village of the New Territories, will enable you to delve into Hong Kong's past. The newly open Hong Kong Museum of Art shows touring exhibitions of masterpieces of Eastern and Western Art, such as the recent collection of paintings by Marc Chagall. Art galleries display works by masters and experimenters. Works of sculpture by Henry Moore dot the urban landscape. It will take time to become acquainted with the museums, but as a resident you will have more than a day or two to explore them. The Friends of the Chinese University Art Gallery and the Friends of the Hong Kong University Museum are particularly active, and welcome residents such as yourself as members. Do not ignore the T T Tsui Museum in the old Bank of China Building.

MUSIC

Chinese vocal and instrumental music is appreciated mostly by an older Chinese audience, especially those newly settled in Hong Kong. All schools of Chinese opera from the different provinces of China tour Hong Kong regularly. Hong Kong has its own Chinese Orchestra; it holds concerts at the Cultural Centre and in halls throughout the territory. Almost three quarters of a million people heard the

85-member orchestra in its 106 concerts during 1993. Chinese music, perhaps much more than Chinese visual art, remains difficult for people not reared in the Chinese tradition to appreciate. However, Chinese instruments are being modernized and will be better attuned to the non-Asian ear. The seating of the players has been modified also, to reflect Western influences. The conductor stands in front of the orchestra with his back to the audience. The number of players has been increased, creating a larger sound to suit the modern concert halls. In 1994 the Chinese Orchestra joined the Hong Kong Philharmonic for a number of joint concerts.

As more and more young people come to appreciate Western music, concerts in Hong Kong are well attended. A large cultural complex was built in Tsimshatsui, housing concert halls, drama theatres and museums. Choral music, traditionally, attracts a large following. Whereas learning an instrument costs money, choral work does not. So music training in Hong Kong schools is principally vocal. The Hong Kong Philharmonic Orchestra, with local and expatriate professional players has, since the 1970s, enjoyed a stormy relationship with several principal conductors. But the orchestra also plays under the batons of world famous guest conductors and soloists. *The Phil*, equally at home with Telemann and Mahler, has toured abroad. Younger local musicians play with the Hong Kong Sinfonietta, which was established in 1991 with support from the Council for the Performing Arts.

Visiting orchestras, ensembles and soloists have Hong Kong firmly on their East Asian tour programmes. Ethnic Chinese musicians who have won renown elsewhere enjoy a warm following here. The most popular of these is Yo Yo Ma. Perhaps it is jet lag, or perhaps unconscious condescension to Hong Kong audiences thought not to be versed in Western music – visitors seem on occasions not to give of their best. Hearing one of the world's most popular tenors in Vienna, for instance, was a heavenly experience. Listening to him here, especially when the concert was given in an arena built for sports, was a test of endurance. But it is not only here that big commercial promotions yield small musical dividends. In dog-Latin, *Circus maximus, ars minimus.*

Eastern European orchestras tour under the jurisdiction of the Regional rather than the Urban Council. They appear in New Territories concert halls, where acoustics range from superb to plain awful. Still, the divided jurisdiction between the municipal councils means that people in all parts of Hong Kong can enjoy good music in their own neighbourhoods.

Amateur music groups perform regularly. The Hong Kong Oratorio Society leads the vocal field, with several concerts each year. The Bach Choir is also excellent, as are groups which put on Gilbert and Sullivan operettas. There are also church choirs and the Hong Kong Philharmonic Chorus. An amateur group specializes in 'ancient' music and 'original' instruments. Depending on your skill and your willingness to commit time, you will be welcomed by any of these groups as player, singer – or listener.

THE ACADEMY OF PERFORMING ARTS

The Academy of Performing Arts was established in 1985 to train Hong Kong students who wish to specialize in performing vocal and instrumental music, dance, theatre – and in technical arts. Now granting diplomas, it is preparing to award degrees in 1995. Located in its exciting building in Wanchai since 1986, there are some six hundred full-time students, and a junior department of eight hundred children who study dance and music part-time. A small post-graduate course in Opera of the Western Tradition started in 1990. Seven students are enrolled in this programme during the 1993–94 academic year. Three are from Shanghai, one from Malaysia, and two from the United Kingdom. Past students have come from Beijing and Australia as well. Fifteen undergraduates are training in voice, and hope to join the Postgraduate Opera programme when they complete their current studies. The Opera Department has performed *La Bohème, Carmen* and *Figaro* in the original languages, with the Academy's orchestra and chorus, to critical and popular acclaim. Sets and costumes were designed by Academy students. Music undergraduates are invited to perform at Government House, and these concerts are open to the public. The Drama Department produces plays principally in Cantonese, while the Dance Department stages American musicals with lyrics translated into Cantonese. The dance graduating class presents an exquisite programme each spring in Hong Kong and Guangzhou.

THEATRE AND DANCE

Repertory and amateur dramatic groups produce plays in English or Cantonese: the Hong Kong Repertory Theatre, the Chung Ying Theatre Company, the Exploration Theatre (which, founded by the American community in 1982, performs original works by local playwrights), the Academy of Performing Arts, and groups at the Fringe. They all perform regularly, and welcome new members with theatrical interests.

Dance *aficionados* and connoisseurs should not feel left out by the Hong Kong cultural scene. The Hong Kong Dance Company performs traditional Chinese dances. The Western genre is represented by the Hong Kong Ballet and the City Contemporary Dance Company. Jean Wong, a ballet dancer and businesswoman originally from Shanghai, runs a string of ballet dance studios throughout the territory, training young men and women in the art of ballet. As a result, the audience for dance grows vigorously. Mary Griffith is here as an 'expatriate spouse'. She holds a master's degree in mathematics and engineering from Oxford, and is trained in ballet. She is able to combine her teaching career as head of the Mathematics Department at the Chinese International School, with ballet lessons as an extra-curricular activity for junior and senior students.

THE HONG KONG ARTS FESTIVAL

For about a month each winter, the Hong Kong Arts Festival attracts all genres of Western and Eastern performing arts to the territory. The Arts Festival has become an established institution in Asia since its founding in 1973. Audiences from abroad join Hong Kong residents in anticipation of this festival. The organizers take into consideration all styles of Hong Kong taste, and seem to know exactly which of the dozen or more locales is suitable for a particular group of performers. The Arts Festival brings in more than a thousand artists from abroad each year. Their programmes include drama in English and Chinese, opera, dance, orchestral and smaller ensemble music, mimes, magicians, Peking and provincial Chinese opera, plus Japanese and other Asian arts. Hong Kong's own Philharmonic Orchestra usually opens and closes the Festival; visiting troupes have included the Royal Shakespeare Company, the Paris Opera Ballet, New York's Ensemble for Early Music, the King's Singers and Japanese Kabuki Theatre. Ticket prices have been held at reasonable levels because the Council for the Performing Arts finds donors through the matching grant scheme. Businesses and individuals sponsor particular performances. Hotels and airlines sponsor lodging and transport. Individual philanthropists subsidize student tickets. Museums and galleries mount special exhibitions within the Arts Festival.

Programmes are announced each September, when you may order tickets by post. Tickets go on sale at the various box offices one month before the events concerned. It is easy to buy tickets in person, because all box offices are linked by something called URBTIX. A message of warning: do not be too enthusiastic and buy more tickets than you will be able to use. A rule of thumb: no more than two events a week – but it is hard to confine oneself to such a regimen.

Besides this major festival there are the annual Asian Arts Festival, film festivals of various kinds and in various languages, and festivals catering to more specialized interests.

ORDERING TICKETS BY TELEPHONE

Telephone reservations means just that. You will still have to collect the tickets from a specified box office. On the telephone you must follow a set procedure. If you say what you want in your own way, you will say it many times. Establish that you want to buy tickets, and wait to be asked step by step what date, which performance, where, the title of the show, how many tickets and at what price. On further prompting, give your name and the numbers of your credit card and your identity card or passport. We are in the age of computers imitating people and *vice versa*. Here the process makes for efficiency. See whether you can match it when, after a day or two, you judge your creditworthiness to have been verified, and go to the right box office with your credentials: credit and identity cards (or passport). You may have to prove you are indeed you, before you receive your tickets.

GAMBLING

Gambling is a way of life in Hong Kong. Sanctioned by law or not, the Chinese bet on horse and dog races, play mahjong and fantan at home, on the street or at small stalls – or in clubs set up for the purpose of gambling – and buy lottery tickets literally by the gross.

Mahjong, a game of tiles played by four people sitting at a table, is a latecomer to Chinese gambling. The game was not played in China until the Ming dynasty. It used to be a social game for the leisured classes, but playing with money makes it more fun. In addition to the winners, people who gain financially from this game are the numerous restaurants catering to mahjong. On weekend evenings the noise from tiles is deafening. Of course we can argue that a peaceful meal at a Chinese restaurant is a contradiction in terms, but no old Hong Kong hand would venture into any such restaurant hoping to enjoy a half-way peaceful dinner. Dominoes, dating back to the Tang dynasty, is a game more ancient than the mahjong; but it is less prestigious. It is played in the street because it is a faster game. The stakes are smaller. The Chinese call this game 'connecting dragons'. The most popular game in Hong Kong is fantan, a card game played by any number of players, with or without a board.

Night racing at Happy Valley.

Royal Hong Kong Jockey Club – Lotteries Fund

Charitable use of the proceeds from gambling began during the administration of Governor Sir Richard Macdonnell, during the late 1860s, with the appropriation of funds or a grant of land to establish the Tung Hua Hospital to take care of indigent sick Chinese. Horse racing had been imported into Hong Kong by the British, and the Chinese immediately cottoned on to the gambling aspect of the 'Sport of Kings'. Royal Jockey Club Charities is now one of the largest single contributors to Hong Kong charities. The 'Mark Six' lotteries are drawn every week. The money not given to the winners swells the Lotteries Fund, which is used to finance welfare services through grants and loans.

SPORTS

There are plenty of facilities for sport and recreation in Hong Kong. You can, however, count on the public facilities being crowded when

157

you want to use them, and on the private facilities being beyond your reach. But still, they are there. The South China Athletic Club is an institution to get to know. Facilities include a driving range, and the prices are comfortable. Here you must practise your sportsmanship before your golf and wait with great perseverance. Cricketers will find kindred souls in the Hong Kong and Kowloon cricket clubs.

As with music, Hong Kong is attracting big names to its tennis, squash and golf tournaments. This means, of course, that the prize is right, but it also indicates that the facilities are of international standard.

There are public swimming pools with good hygienic standards. To sail, water ski or snorkel, however, you will need to spend a great deal of money.

Country Parks and Other Walks

Hiking in the country is a noteworthy Chinese tradition which you may wish to adopt. Its cost is low and, except when washed out by rain, the trails are there all the time. 'Get a good map and stay on the trail' is the Government's advice to walkers. The best known, and the most demanding, of the country walks is the MacLehose Trail. Going east and west, the trail is a hundred kilometres long. It is not for novice walkers. But novices will find many easier roads and trails, throughout the green parts of the territory.

There are historic walks in the urban areas. Hong Kong Tourist Association publications give you a wide variety of choice, according to your interests and inclination. Whatever you choose, do not forget the Maipo Marshes – a nature reserve run by the Worldwide Fund for Nature. This sanctuary, on the border between Hong Kong and the People's Republic of China, is the last stopping place for migratory birds from as far away as Siberia and Mongolia on their way to Australia. WWF is one of the agencies seriously trying to protect and improve Hong Kong's environment.

CONCLUSION

Whatever the reason or reasons for your presence in Hong Kong, you will be working hard. If you conscientiously plan some of your leisure, you will be able to enjoy a variety of unexpected activities, without the nuisance of flying away for long holiday weekends. And you will avoid the ultimate misfortune: leaving with half of Hong Kong's character still hidden from you.

— Chapter Seven —

TWO MAJOR HONG KONG INSTITUTIONS – EATING OUT AND SHOPPING

So, these are the real reasons behind your decision to come to Hong Kong – the urge to enjoy Chinese food, and the instinct to shop until you drop.

You can go to restaurants by yourselves, or with non-Cantonese speaking friends, in the urban areas where English-language menus abound. As time goes by, learn to speak at least some Cantonese, by whatever means, and try the restaurants in out-of-the-way places. When you have achieved merely a few polite words and phrases, you will find a warm welcome everywhere. The Hong Kong people may giggle at your pronunciation and intonation, but underneath they will be so appreciative that you are trying to learn their language. It shows that you respect the local people and that you want to be their friends.

At least you will be providing them with something to talk about for days to come. Nowhere will you see more evidence of their appreciation of your linguistic efforts than in the restaurants and shops you decide to patronize.

EATING OUT

Hong Kong people probably eat out more often than those of any other land. There are over thirty thousand restaurants in Hong Kong. All major cuisines of the world are represented: French, Italian, Mediterranean, Indian, Japanese and Korean, for instance; and all schools of Chinese cooking, such as Cantonese, Chiuchow, Sichuan, Shanghainese, Pekingese and Yangzhou. Prices vary from the bank-breaking top of the market to fast food for less than twenty Hong Kong dollars per head. Happily, most of the restaurants come somewhere between. If you want to start with a safe bet, that long-standing institution, Jimmy's Kitchen, has branches on either side of the harbour.

Eating at an open-air restaurant, where the atmosphere is casual and prices are reasonable. All Hong Kong families eat out.

There have been substantial rises in lower to middle incomes during the last dozen years: not enough to pay for luxury cars or foreign holidays, but enabling families to eat well and often in Hong Kong restaurants. Certainly some people eat out only once in a while, as a birthday treat or some other celebration; but there are people who eat all three meals in restaurants every day. Hong Kong parents do not appear to need to adjust their schedules to their children's bed-times, so you see whole families eating out even on weekdays.

Haute Cuisine to Fast Food, Western Style

The large number of Western restaurants reflects the cosmopolitan character of Hong Kong. Consult the young men and women in the international business world for insight into Hong Kong's eateries. There will be no cultural shock when you eat in these restaurants; apart from the Chinese appearance of the waiters and waitresses, there is nothing to suggest that you are in such a far away place as Hong Kong.

It is taken for granted that better Western food can be found in its native countries, but there is no need to apologize for the chefs of Hong Kong. That stand-by of many years, Gaddi's at the Peninsula; or the Hilton and the Mandarin Grills; and relative newcomers to the scene, Petrus at the Island Shangri-la or Nicholini's at the Conrad: these cannot be surpassed in the quality of food, wine, ambience and service. In fact, luxury hotels try to out-perform each other in their Western and their Chinese cuisines, and you can benefit from their competition. It is difficult for restaurants serving Western food to operate other than in hotels because of the high rents, but a number do provide exceptional food and thrive: such as Cafe Damigo in Happy Valley or M at the Fringe. Prices in all restaurants have risen in recent years, but there are set-luncheon menus which should not offend either your pocketbook or your sense of fairness.

At the lower end, fast food has become a fad in Hong Kong. It is astonishing how the Chinese, who traditionally rejected both tomatoes and cheese, have taken to pizza, over-cooked hamburgers and french fries – in Hong Kong. This open expression of fondness for Western food is no longer solely a status symbol with which Hong Kong people try to show their modernity. They actually like these new-fangled comestibles. Sandwiches, however, are still thought of as snack food, not as a substitute for rice or noodles in a main meal.

Chinese Restaurants

It is almost impossible to find bad Cantonese food in Hong Kong. The Chinese restaurants, large and small, up-market or basic, all serve edible food, and more than a few serve great food. A number of restaurants have adopted the chic of *nouvelle cuisine*, arranging the food exquisitely to Western aesthetic standards; and many have given up *maijin* – monosodium glutumate, the chemical taste-enhancer that causes the *Chinese Restaurant Syndrome* of burning headaches and swelling limbs, symptoms which received widespread publicity in Europe and America a while ago. It is perfectly acceptable to ask the waiter to leave out the *maijin*. More likely than not the chef will bow to your wishes since the cost of *maijin*, imported from Japan, is on the high side. Make sure that the cook is asked to leave out chicken essence also, which is used as a substitute for *maijin*. If you read the contents on a chicken essence bottle, the first item you see will be *maijin*.

There is a newly opened chain of moderately priced restaurants serving substantial Cantonese food, albeit a little heavy on *maijin*. It is known for its soups and casseroles; indeed, the name of the restaurants is Ah Yee Liang Tong, literally meaning *Number Two's Terrific Soup*. Shirleen Ho tells the traditional story that Ah Yee, meaning Number Two, was the euphemism for a man's mistress, his wife being Number One. When the man visited the Number Two he had to eat something; but if he partook of a full meal his wife would suspect that he had eaten somewhere else, when his appetite was not up to its usual standard. And, if this state of affairs continued, the wife would know that he had a second household. Hence, he could only accede to the soup course at Number Two's, and the Number Two, of pleasing nature by definition, learned to make terrific soup.

Expatriate residents like to patronize a couple of large Pekingese restaurants where the noise is beyond tolerance but where good food is offered at reasonable prices. They also like the Sichuanese restaurants which offer almost exactly the same menu as certain other Sichuanese restaurants – say in New York's Upper East Side. There is nothing wrong with these restaurants, but you should try others also.

EATING WITH CHOPSTICKS

You must learn as soon as possible to eat with chopsticks. The restaurants will provide you with knife and fork but, unless you suffer from arthritis, it is difficult to explain why a Hong Kong resident cannot handle chopsticks. You will learn easily and, once you have, it is like riding a bicycle: the skill is yours forever. On the other hand, it is better to be safe than sorry. Until you have mastered the art of eating with chopsticks, ask for the Western implements. Dry-cleaning is not as readily available as you might like and, as with the price of a silk tie, dry-cleaning costs have risen into the stratosphere.

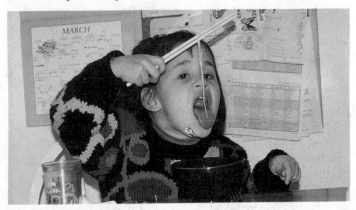

You cannot start too young: this Eurasian child has the hang of it … in her own fashion.

A Chinese host and his guests toast one another – and the delicious food.

The Etiquette of Restaurant Dining, Family Style

Your Chinese friends and business acquaintances rarely entertain at home. Unless they live in spacious quarters and enjoy the services of a good cook, they will invite you to dine at one of Hong Kong's many excellent restaurants serving Chinese food, some of which are in private clubs. It is not that they want to keep you out of their personal space, as with a stranger; but they might worry about losing face should you not like their home, or feel that it is too humble.

Entertaining in Chinese restaurants may take place in the general dining room, where it is less formal and where food is ordered from a regular menu. You will be asked by your host to choose something from this menu. Unless you know your host very well, let him order. The chances are that he will not select anything that is too exotic, unless he knows specifically that you are partial to duck's tongue or *brèche de mer*. If you are truly allergic to certain types of food, speak up and be absolutely firm that you cannot 'try a little bit' under any circumstances. You will be eating *family-style* in the sense that all the dishes will be for everyone to share. The dishes will be placed in the middle of the table, and all of you will be serving yourselves from them, unless the host takes this task upon himself or a waitress or waiter officiates.

Dipping your chopsticks into the serving bowl with aplomb when you dine with a family – or in the same style with any group – is going to be hard. (For a while, kind people will understand your difficulty and indulge you, as if you were not quite grown up.) Even harder to become accustomed to is everybody else at the table dipping into the same bowl with chopsticks which have been in and out of their mouths. However, standards of hygiene are beginning to take priority over the intimacy of sharing a meal family-style. Note that when your host serves his guests, he turns the chopsticks around, so that the ends that have been in his mouth does not touch the food he is giving you. When you serve yourself, turn your chopsticks around too, and pick up the food you want with the other ends. It is all right to reach across the table, but choose the piece of food closest to you. For more than three score years reformers have been trying to introduce 'common chopsticks' for serving purposes, but have enjoyed little success. Most of the food will have been cut into bite sizes already. It is perfectly in order to bite into larger pieces with your front teeth, as long as you do not drag the portion that has been in your mouth out and onto your plate again.

The Etiquette of Being Entertained in a Private Room

Alternatively you might be entertained in a private dining room, reserved for your party alone. This is banquet dining, on a small scale. Food is ordered from a special menu in advance, and the meal is a great deal more expensive than in the general dining room. It is understood that shark's fin will be a part of the meal in private room dining. In a Cantonese restaurant, the meal will also include steamed whole garoupa or preserved abalone; in a Pekingese restaurant, the ubiquitous roast duck with pancakes.

In any case, in order to justify the specialized service and the privacy of the dining room, you are expected to drink alcohol, sodas or *fresh* orange juice; not merely water or tea. Whatever you order to drink will keep on coming all evening, unless you stop the waiter or waitress firmly. A word of warning must be added here. Fresh orange juice may look appetizing, but since it was squeezed many more than fifteen minutes before, all the vitamins will have disappeared before it reaches you, leaving only sugar. Somehow a persuasive salesman has managed to convince the Hong Kong public that a certain brand of distilled water is good for your health, so it is served everywhere, including hospitals where there are heart patients. If you do not wish to become a part of this scheme of drinking water without any character or mineral content, order boiled tap water. Your host will probably bring along a bottle of brandy, which he and the guests will drink neat, or have a bottle with his name on it already at the restaurant, indicating that he is a regular patron: another status symbol, to be noticed by the initiated. The territory boasts the highest per capita consumption of cognac outside France; nowadays, the status of the cognac is no longer determined by the number of stars on the bottle, but by the presence or absence of the letters XO.

The guest of honour is always seated furthest from the door. Today, men and women are usually seated at the same table, assuming that both sexes are represented. If so, your spouse will be seated next to you. Traditionally, Chinese women and men were seated in separate rooms or at separate tables; by putting spouses together, it is hoped that the guest wife will feel less awkward at this gathering of strangers. The host will be seated closest to the door. It will always be a round table, in the middle of which a 'lazy susan' keeps the food circulating. When the waiter or waitress handles the serving, an equal portion of every dish will be placed on a small plate, and yours will be placed in front of you. There is no need to eat the whole lot unless you truly like it; and remember that there are at least ten courses at these dinners in a private dining room. Few diners have risen hungry from a Chinese banquet table. To reduce the chances of such a misfortune, the last course is apt to be the heaviest, but not necessarily the least interesting. The meal is over when the waiter places a bowl of flowers in the middle of the lazy susan. It is your cue to get up and say good night, if you are the guest of honour. Do not linger.

During the meal, the courses will be served one at a time. As your host gestures you to start eating, by extending his chopsticks and saying 'Please', you should raise your cup or glass and say 'Thank you' before you eat. Confucius has always been quoted as saying that one does not talk while one is eating, and no doubt your mother would agree with him. In other words, do not talk with your mouth full. In between courses, of course, there will be conversation. After all, you have been invited to dinner so that you and your host can get to know each other less formally than across the desks of your offices. You will find, however, that only the guest of honour and the host exchange pleasantries. If you are junior to your host, do not speak unless addressed directly; and remember that serious subjects are rarely brought up. Please note especially that this is neither the time nor the place to show off your command of Cantonese, unless you speak it really well and the host has asked you to use the language. Nor is it considered macho any more to drink too much alcohol.

The Feast Menu

At first, everything on the table will be new and exotic to you. Give it a try, you may like it. In time, you may become blasé and enjoy each dish for the texture and the flavour. Some things will never lose their appeal even after many years. An occasional Peking Duck is still exciting to behold, and even sweet-and-sour pork does not lose its freshness. Actually, the most unusual items on the menu will probably be shark's fin and perhaps a whole roast piglet with head and tail. If you recognize the solitary brownish oval-shaped object on a plate as preserved abalone, and if you do not want to struggle with this rubbery delicacy, feel free to decline. As they cost a thousand or more dollars apiece, the host is sure to forgive you for not taking one bite and leaving the rest on the plate. When you espy chrysanthemum petals, however, it is time to focus positively on what is being served. These flower petals always accompany snake soup. Snake soup is considered a nourishing delicacy during the winter months. It is harmless, and moderately expensive, so it would not be a polite gesture to decline.

At such meals in Hong Kong today, the bill of fare is usually on the table in both Chinese and English, so that you will know what you are eating. Still, you may find the following poem entertaining. It was penned by a Western trader at Canton, W C Hunter, who was given what appeared to be a sumptuous Cantonese feast by a Chinese merchant, and harboured his own private fears as one dish was uncovered after another. The poem was printed in *The 'Fan Kwae' at Canton Before Treaty Days 1825–1844* (London, 1882).

The feast spread out, the splendour round
Allowed the eye no rest;
The wealth of Kwang-Tung, of all Ind,
Appeared to greet each guest.

All tongues are still; no converse free
The solemn silence broke.
Because, alas! friend Se-Ta-Che [Western guest]
No word of Chinese spoke.

Now here, now there, he picked a bit
Of what he could not name;
And all he knew was that, in fact,
They made him sick the same!

Mingqua, his host, pressed on each dish
With polished Chinese grace;

And much, Ming thought, he relished them,
At every ugly face!

At last he swore he'd eat no more,
'Twas written in his looks;
For, 'Zounds!' said he, 'the devil here
Sends both the meats and cooks!'

But, covers changed, he brightened up,
And thought himself in luck
When close before him, what he saw
Looked something like a duck!

Still cautious grown, but, to be sure,
His brain he set to rack;
At length he turned to one behind,
And, pointing, cried: 'Quack, Quack.'

The Chinese gravely shook his head,
Next made a reverend bow;
And then expressed what dish it was
By uttering, 'Bow-wow-wow!'

The Teahouse: a Great Hong Kong Tradition

Yum cha literally means *drinking tea*, or *to drink tea* when used as a verb. After thousands of years of tea connoisseurship the Chinese have yet to come up with a dripless spout. However, despite the introduction of coffee, soda and other beverages, tea drinking has remained an important tradition. Teahouses have existed in China since antiquity, serving a variety of teas, generally with watermelon seeds, or peanuts in their shells. It was the Cantonese who first introduced food into the teahouses; they became known as *yum cha* or *dim sum* restaurants. The food served in the teahouses never amounted to major meals, only *dim sum*: literally small pieces of meat or vegetable wrapped in pastry and easily eaten. Although *yum cha* and *dim sum* are used synonymously in Hong Kong, there is, properly, a distinction – when you go to a restaurant to *yum cha*, you eat *dim sum;* or, when you *yum cha*, you drink tea and eat *dim sum.*

Until recently, before tablecloths were introduced into *yum cha* restaurants, women used to pushcarts of *dim sum* among the tables and sing out what was on their individual carts. The patrons indicated what they wanted by asking – or gesturing with their hands or their chins – which added to the informality of the atmosphere. Today, there is an order form (often bilingual) on the table for you to fill in with what you want to eat; or your order is taken by a uniformed waiter. The food is no less delicious, but *à la carte* is not so much fun as from the cart. During the past decade, *dim sum* prices have risen more than tenfold.

Dim sum restaurants in Hong Kong are informal places where business news is gathered and transactions are made. Certain restaurants are patronized by certain trades or professions. Property owners, for instance, meet at the Luk Yew Teahouse and have a table reserved for them every day. This is why in general there is no space for a casual customer until after two-thirty. The Chinese way of making a business deal is not to negotiate in the presence of a legal team, but to talk about items of mutual interest in an informal place over tea and *dim sum*. Introductions are made and people and business are brought together. This old way of conducting business is also on the way out, as younger generations and hired managers take over.

THE GREAT CHEFS OF HONG KONG

Perhaps the most efficient and least costly way to sample the best international and Chinese cuisines is at a Los Angeles institution transplanted here, the *Great Chefs* of Hong Kong. It takes place each year at the Hilton Hotel Ballroom as a fund-raising event, thanks to the generosity of the hotel and its indefatigable general manager James Smith.

Pushing the dim sum *cart. She calls out what she has on board, and you point to what you want to eat. Sadly, this is a dying tradition.*

More than twenty hotels and restaurants support their chefs in donating talent, time and special dishes to benefit the Heep Hong Society for Handicapped Children. In 1993, cuisines of the Australian, Austrian, Californian, Cantonese, French, German, Italian, Japanese, New Zealand, Swiss and Thai schools were represented at the *Great Chefs*: as truly international a collection of delicious mouthfuls as you can hope to eat standing up.

Champagne, still wines, mineral water, *espresso* coffee – and more – flow through the largesse of their local distributors. These included a Hong Kong Chinese architect educated at Harvard, and an Austrian lawyer trained in Vienna, serving beverages themselves in their inimitable styles and adding much to the convivial atmosphere of the occasion. Patrons walk around the Ballroom, drinking and eating what they want. If you would like a particular chef to cook a meal for you and your friends at home, you can bid for his or, indeed, her services at the auction that is a part of the *Great Chefs*. This grand charity function is open to the general public.

Alas, plans are being made to demolish the hotel and replace it with an office building; so, by the time you read this book, *Great Chefs* will probably be looking for another host.

SHOPPING IN HONG KONG

Shopping in Hong Kong is no longer confined to hunting for bargains or counterfeit merchandise, or picking up a Chinese curio or two. In fact, there are few great bargains left. But as a resident you can find almost anything you need if you spend time and energy looking for it. Maybe you will not be able to locate a dozen maroon-coloured bath towels all at once; but you can accumulate all the ingredients you need for baking a Christmas fruit cake by visiting three or four special food shops – Seibu, Oliver's, USA and Company – or even your local supermarket.

Service standards in Hong Kong, especially in shops frequented by tourists, have improved vastly during the past decade, although

NOT for the cake: this shop sells dried sea creatures – squid, scallops, shrimps and oysters, for instance.

A stall in Stanley (a district where expatriates like to live) selling fresh fruit and some vegetables.

here and there you may still face surly assistants – unless they have deduced somehow that you are about to spend a great deal of money. Following this line of thought, Japanese tourists are in general served first in the boutiques with the most elevated prices. You can always walk out in a huff if you are not thought to be Japanese. Otherwise if that particular shop stocks what you really desire, you will just have to persevere until you have secured the full attention of the staff and cajoled from them the merchandise you want to see. The staff are mostly young and underpaid women whose command of English is at best hesitant, and whose self-assurance comes with the uniforms they wear. When all else fails, ask to speak with the manager.

Yes, there are unscrupulous shopkeepers in Hong Kong. Victims may have recourse to the Hong Kong Consumers' Council. The best way to approach any purchase of substance – whether a camera, a fax machine, a watch, or a diamond necklace – is to get someone who has been here for some time and has established *guanxi* (a special relationship) with certain shopkeepers, to go with you. You can then be more sure that you are buying a genuine article at a fair price.

The Shopping Malls

The one place in Hong Kong that may make you feel at home is the shopping mall, if you are used to these standard facilities; but the Hong Kong malls have a distinct character of their own. There are restaurants, yes, including McDonalds and other fast food emporia, department stores and a variety of specialist shops, but the merchandise in the shops will be more international than you find at home. The advent of up-market malls – Galleria, Landmark and Pacific Place – featuring the most elegant of shops, has led to the up-grading of older malls such as Ocean Terminal. There are other large malls, the Shatin Plaza and those at Taikooshing and Times Square, for instance, which cater to a less well-heeled clientele. These malls also serve as air-conditioned indoor playgrounds for family outings at weekends and holidays, especially when the weather is too hot or too wet out of

Not a shopping mall, but a warehouse shop. An expatriate family buys essentials, in the latest way.

doors. There are exhibits, concerts and, lately, fashion shows to entertain lunch-time and weekend shoppers and sightseers. The Taikooshing mall even boasts an ice-skating rink.

Etiquette of Street Hawkers and Bargain Emporia

There are still factory outlets throughout Hong Kong, but you should be prepared to pick through a lot of imperfect factory rejects under the watchful eyes of untrusting proprietors. The sound of Cantopop is beyond the normal level of tolerance; but, if you know what you are looking for and know your labels, the prices are really superb. Stanley has become too chic for good bargains, but newcomers and visitors still find the market exciting. The etiquette allows bargaining. However, confronted with a proprietress with a cunning eye for profit, you are not going to get very far. The rules also allow you all the time you want to investigate the goods in the fixed premises but, since hawking on the street without a licence is illegal, partly because many items are

Hawker stalls on an uncrowded day. Like the shoppers and browsers, the advertising is mainly but not wholly Chinese.

counterfeit, you need to rush when you negotiate with a mobile hawker. Once money is paid to a proprietress or a hawker, goods can neither be exchanged nor returned.

Antiques, Curios, Souvenirs and Junk

Hong Kong specializes in Chinese antiques, curios, souvenirs and junk. Sometimes it takes a knowledgeable eye or a trusted dealer to tell them apart. Usually the only items you will find made for non-Chinese taste are the China Trade pieces – things made in China for sale abroad or to Westerners who lived in China.

There are antique dealers in the shopping malls and other elegant establishments, including hotel arcades, but nothing has taken away the romance and adventure of hunting for antiques in Hollywood Road and its environs. If any object made a century or more ago is

177

considered an antique (as defined by the United States Customs), then there are a great many genuine antiques in Hong Kong, from neolithic pottery to late Qing furniture, all available for purchase. You must remember, however, that age and value do not always go hand in hand. There are even more objects – better labelled as curios, souvenirs and junk – that pose as antiques. Follow the advice of the Tourist Association: patronize only stores sporting the HKTA logo. At least these antique dealers will not lie about the age and value of the piece that happens to attract your eye. No true connoisseur buys on sight without investigation; that is, long drawn-out discussions with dealers about date and origin – but not necessarily provenance – and of course price.

Real antiques that you fancy might not be as expensive as you expect. Rare treasures, of course, command prices beyond ordinary pockets like yours or mine; and are auctioned at Christie's or Sotheby's, both of which maintain offices in Hong Kong. Chinese tastes in

Tourists being shown curios and junk on Cat Street near Hollywood Road at the heart of Hong Kong's antiques trade.

antiques differ from those of expatriates, which is fortunate for you. Whereas you think a pottery figure pretty exciting – say, a fat lady in green and yellow glaze excavated from a Tang dynasty tomb – Chinese collectors would prefer not to own something intended for the dead. Neolithic pottery jars are no longer a dime a dozen but, because there are so many of them on the Hong Kong market, the prices are still affordable.

Expatriate residents in Hong Kong seem to have a partiality for Korean chests, and indeed these are lovely and are available everywhere, but most of them were manufactured in your lifetime. Go browsing in Hollywood Road and Wyndham Street when you have time. The antique shops are mostly family owned and managed. The dealers know and love their wares. Genuine collectors spend Saturday afternoons there, establishing *guanxi* with their favourite antique dealers. The dealers, many of whom speak excellent English, enjoy sharing their passion with the true connoisseur. Once in a while, however, you are expected to buy.

Clothing

The availability of ready-made apparel for men and women, and the rise in labour costs, have brought about the decline of clothing 'tailor-made in Hong Kong'. When European designers embarked on the course of producing more than one costume per design, Hong Kong jumped onto their bandwagon. When you can buy off the rack from boutiques featuring a selection of the world's most renowned names – which can provide you with style as well as a symbol of status – why would you subject yourself to some anonymous tailor who demands at least four fittings? Good tailors are still around, of course, but they are expensive. Those who have not yet emigrated are getting old, and no younger generation wielding a mighty needle has yet emerged to take their places. More affordable clothing can be found in Japanese department stores and boutiques, featuring garments made in Asia; and in the Chinese emporia selling clothes made in

China. In general the Hong Kong population is conscious of the latest trends in style, and dresses well.

One area which has seen improvement in recent years in the retail rag trade is larger-sized clothing for the fuller non-Chinese figure. It is difficult to keep your cool when the saleswomen tell you that they do not stock clothes for fat people – extra offensive if said in Cantonese because the dialect uses the same adjective for fat people and fat animals. Or, if 'extra-large' sizes were offered, these would fit your eleven-year-old child. Happily, this kind of humiliation has come to an end. There are shops which cater for large men and women, though you have to look for them. Again, you will need to consult the grapevine.

Watches, Jewellery and Electronic Bargains of Yore

Once more, develop your own *guanxi* in shops that carry watches, jewellery, cameras and electronic bargains of yesteryear. The best way is for a friend already enjoying such a relationship to introduce you. You may then hope for the best possible prices without being cheated. The practice of unscrupulous traders trying to get rid of their out-of-date if not altogether bogus merchandise on unsuspecting customers is most prevalent in these markets. Distrust all 'great deals'. Always see that there is a guarantee as well as a warranty. Anything that needs plugging into an electric outlet should be scrutinized to ensure worldwide use, because dual voltage appliances should be universal today, except perhaps in Japan and the United States where appliances are available for the single voltage of 110–120.

Computers – Plus Software and Computer Games

All makes of computer, including IBM personal computers and Apple products, are available in Hong Kong. Clones made in Asia are also here, as is much pirated hardware and software. You will have to examine your conscience when you venture into the labyrinth of bargain computer supplies: Government agents still raid the shops from time to time for counterfeits. Be prepared to pay heavily for service and replacement parts. The facts that many young school children play hand-held computer games during break instead of kicking a ball, and that Triad-controlled computer game parlours can be found in various neighbourhoods, are of increasing concern to educational and law enforcement authorities.

CASH, CREDIT CARDS AND DISCOUNTS

Almost all your guidebooks tell you to bargain in Hong Kong. Indeed, bargaining was a part of the fun of shopping. Modernization of business practices, however, has led to the installation of price tags on all kinds of merchandise. Even so, most stores will give you a discount if you insist, and jewellers will give a higher discount than, say, Lane Crawford. Usually, discounts apply to cash sales only. Cheques used to be accepted everywhere, but since the advent of credit cards, paying by personal cheque is a thing of the past. A rule of thumb is: if the sales staff are surly and the service is bad, use whichever credit card takes the highest percentage for commission. When all else fails, bring someone skilful at handling recalcitrant shop assistants with you.

CONCLUSION

In the long run people who live in Hong Kong can keep their shopping to a minimum; but eating out is another and a pleasanter matter.

— Chapter Eight —

GETTING READY FOR LIFE IN HONG KONG

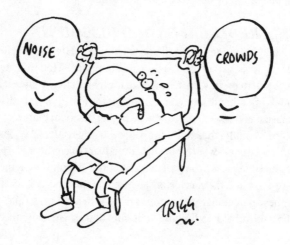

At this point you may think that you have made a major mistake in deciding to move here. The complexity of the Hong Kong environment cannot be overemphasized. A result of historical development, this complexity can be seen as a foundation of strong Chinese values under the authority of a British administration, topped with a veneer of cosmopolitanism which comes from being a major centre of international business. Here we offer descriptions and pointers to cushion and guide you through the maze. In Hong Kong more than anywhere, we believe newcomers need such informative insights as a *Culture Shock!* absorber.

Before we undertake an extensive discussion of the values embedded in the Hong Kong ethos, a few comments about adjustment as a process should be made. We shall describe three phases, and five stages, of adjustment. While these phases and stages are not mutually exclusive, we shall discuss them separately.

Three Phases of Change

When you leave one situation to enter another, you must go through these three phases of the adjustment process. The first phase is the ending of what has been your life; the second is the 'space' between; and the third is the beginning of your new life.

Probably you are going to work abroad for the first time. As you hand over your responsibilities to your successor, there is a great deal of stress, and perhaps relief. There are the physical activities of moving out of one residence, perhaps selling a house which you have made into a family home and in which you have accumulated objects – part junk, part things you love and part both. Your children need your understanding and support as they take leave of their schools and friends. Then there are the social activities at which your colleagues, neighbours, friends and relatives say farewell. After all that, you arrive in Hong Kong and you are looking forward to what promises to be an excitingly new life. If you have done your homework, you know what to expect.

It is interesting to recognize that while people undergo the experience, as you are doing, they expend time and energy thinking about the first and the third phases of their move; but they often neglect the transitional phase, or take it so much for granted that its passage is hardly noticed. Perhaps this is because the phase is only transitory, in the sense that it does not last very long. A person changing jobs in the West may be expected to take only the two-day weekend between leaving the old job on a Friday and starting the new one on Monday. Here in Hong Kong no distances are involved, and we work on Saturday mornings; so the period of transition between two jobs may well be as brief as a day and a half. How long a person really *needs*, to move from the old situation to the new, depends on the individual. If the transitional phase is ignored, the shock he might experience later could be severe in inverse proportion to the time taken to adjust. The period of transition can be likened to the split second when a trapeze artist lets go of one swing, executes a fancy turn, and hopes that the other swing is in place for him to grasp. With thorough preparation and precision timing, the danger of an accident can be minimized.

In the days when people changed hemispheres by sea, one became an expatriate imperceptibly as the ship glided round the globe. If a move to Hong Kong implied a big transition, then the voyage gave ample time for this middle phase. In making it physically possible to go from old desk to new over the weekend, Hong Kong style, the aeroplane has much to answer for psychologically.

Five Stages of Adjustment

It is useful to overlay the five stages of adjustment to the new situation on those three phases, as we examine them. The stages are: 1) 'Honeymoon' 2) 'Not like home' 3) 'Different, but how?' 4) 'Learn about the differences' and 5) 'Accept them'. You might think that all the adjustment belongs to the third phase – that learning is 'on the job'. But awareness of the changes comes a lot more quickly than your emotional adjustment; though the speed of your practical grasp hides the slowness of your mind and heart. To put it technically, a dysfunction may result from these different paces of adjustment – leading to an 'after shock', unpleasant in itself and likely to slow your progress through the three later stages.

The first stage of adjustment often resembles a honeymoon where everything is new and exciting. Time is usually filled with busy activities related to getting ready for the new environment. There is so much that demands attention that you will hardly find time to miss what you have left behind. You need to unpack, first of all, and get to your office to start the new job. There are new people to meet and new routines to learn. Or, if you are the spouse, you will need to glean practical information on living in Hong Kong; for instance, where you will shop for groceries, or where you can find an electrician. You will also have to make sure that the children are adjusting to their new school and are making new friends.

Once new daily routines have been established and superficial adjustments have been made, feelings of missing the old and familiar will surface. One may resent ways in which Hong Kong is not 'just like home'. At this, the second stage, you may behave untypically: by complaining, becoming easily irritable, lacking energy, experiencing difficulties in focusing on what you should be doing, and so forth. Instead of enjoying what is available, you concentrate on what is not. The duration of this stage depends on the original state and balance of one's mental health. Nevertheless, no matter how severely this stage has affected you, there is no need to make matters worse by worrying. You shall overcome: if not on your own, then with the help of professional people in Hong Kong trained to resolve such difficulties.

The movement from the second to the third stage is signalled by signs of awareness of the differences between the two cultures. One's reaction now is often to reject the strange culture in overt anger. These second and third stages are critical to move through; progress towards stage four is the beginning of recovery.

Stage four starts when you decide to invest time and energy in learning about Hong Kong – and perhaps begin also to analyze the differences between here and where you were. Increasing self-confidence makes a more tranquil mind. At this point, support and reinforcement are needed as you adjust to new behaviour patterns. It is very useful now to have a mentor – what anthropologists call a 'cultural guide' – to serve as a sounding board and validate some of your assumptions. You may do well to take the role of 'participative observer' at this point, when your involvement in activities is just enough to experience the surroundings while leaving you sufficiently detached to analyze the experience.

What you achieve in stage four is fundamental to reaching your goal: acceptance of and participation in the fascinating culture of Hong Kong. That is stage five; and we hope you get there. For you will then be glad of your chance to enjoy the opportunities and pleasures provided by this unique patch of territory and by the people who give it its character.

HONG KONG VALUES AND BELIEFS

The values and beliefs operating within Hong Kong's culture are often deceptive, as you will appreciate after reading the earlier chapters of this book. The external modernity often misleads new-comers into believing 'Oh, it is just like such and such a country' which they already know. Many expatriates voice the conviction that they will have no trouble in feeling at home in Hong Kong. After all, it is not like Beijing or Tokyo; English is in use here. However, as interactions with the Hong Kong culture increase, they begin to feel that something is not quite right, though they seem unable to put a finger on the problem. The Hong Kong Chinese may appear modern and indeed almost Western to the newcomer, because they do indeed speak English, and because they are dressed in the height of interna-tional fashion; but it will not be long before you discover that much is not what it seems. We must describe and analyze for you the fundamental values at work in Hong Kong society.

The Concept of Reciprocity

Hong Kong, like many Asian societies, places more emphasis on the interests of the collective whole than on those of its individuals. In behavioural terms, taking initiatives, being too outspoken or express-ing personal opinions strongly, can be perceived as disturbing the harmony of the whole. The concepts of *face*, and of the networked-self – *maijiang* and *guanxi* – solidify the web of relationships. *Maijiang*, literally meaning the *selling of credit*, is used when a person gives or is given face and when reciprocity is implicitly understood and expected. For instance, if a person has done something for you in some way, you are expected to do something for him in return. It does not mean that you pay him in cash, nor does the return favour have to take place immediately, but the account must be settled one way or another at one time or another. *Guanxi*, literally meaning the *interconnected system* or, in current English-language jargon, *networking*, is the base upon which a person can judge whether he has the right to ask for face. In other words, whether the relationship between the asker and the giver is such that the one can ask without the other having to lose face himself by saying no. Rather, the Chinese do not say no; they just do not say anything when they mean no. In this process, the individual belonging to a certain circle invests time, effort and favour – and so accumulates credit over a long span, occasionally extending through generations.

The Cantonese expressions *yau sum* and *sikdjo,* meaning respectively *having lots of heart* and *understanding what needs to be done,* are often used by the recipient as a form of recognition that a favour has been performed on his behalf. Either term can also be interpreted as a form of thanks or as an indication that the news would be spread through the grapevine. Norms of behaviour in these groups are set through unspoken rules and built-in reinforcement mechanisms. The players automatically comply with the rule, whether it concerns lunch on a certain day of the week, exchange of certain information, the handling of birthday and other celebrations in a certain manner, or the monetary value of gifts. Today, in some instances, especially in gift giving, the process has been simplified to speed and reduce 'accounting' activities. As older generations pass from the scene, such relaxations are easier.

This accounting process still involves exact registrations somewhere, in invisible mental ledgers. It is important to note the value of the present given to your son when he was married so that you can give back the equivalent when the giver's son marries. If reciprocity is broken, it could be interpreted either as the person who breaks the chain feeling that these activities are a waste of time, or as perceiving himself to be superior to this particular accounting system. Of course, if you are a *gweilo*, a foreigner, you do not have to comply; but if you are of the Chinese tradition, you are expected to know and act accordingly. In some instances, these activities can be registered under the category of *li,* which means *ceremonial precepts*, a prescribed way of conduct that has been passed down since ancient times. Special holidays are the time to pay back favours you still have outstanding, and to visit in person the people who are important in your circle of influence.

This giving of gifts, or calling on people, is a form of acknowledgement; it is significant in certain social groups, but it can be carried to ridiculous extremes. For example, some individuals go as far as to measure themselves and their self-worth in terms of how many mooncakes they receive from certain people during the Mid-Autumn Festival. Importance is attached to the standing of the givers of these mooncakes. In the Western tradition, it is important for the boss to buy Christmas or Hanukkah presents for his employees. Under the traditional system of gift giving in Hong Kong, it is the other way round: it is the employer, or the father figure, who must not fail to receive; and the gifts are judged according to their value. Since compliance at an appropriate level is in effect mechanical, it is definitely not the thought that counts.

CHINESE SOCIAL RELATIONSHIPS

A precise hierarchy implicit in the five-fold cardinal relationships described by Confucius, the *wu lun*, provides the strong foundation of the Chinese social order. These five relationships are those between sovereign and subject, father and son, elder brother and younger brother, husband and wife, and between friend and friend.

It is important to note here that there are in Hong Kong certain old families whose position has been established in society for at least three generations – by virtue of wealth ancestrally established. Since their achievements were commercial rather than scholarly, their standards have been taken from what they perceived to be Confucian traditions rather than from any real understanding of the philosophy. This has led to a great deal of uncomprehending inflexibility.

Filial Piety

In Hong Kong's familial relations, *xiao*, or filial piety, the way the children must behave towards the parents is – to use modern terminology – embedded within the collective consciousness. It makes no difference whether a person uses the latest laptop computer or has studied nuclear physics, the *xiao* programme for relating to his family will appear on the screen of his subconscious – and everyone will act accordingly. Filial piety is more than showing respect for the parents, grandparents and all in the family who are one's seniors: it involves care, as well as catering to their wishes and whims. Care, that is, in the sense of affectionate regard; and ultimately therefore in the sense of succour. Conflicts arise when the wishes and whims of the elders are not accepted by the younger generation or – worse – when members of the younger generation become pawns in the elders' games of power play.

There is another side to the *xiao* which is often confusing and contradictory in modern life. The concept of the extended family in feudal and agrarian societies worked well. As the workforce becomes more mobile, and economies become more complex, some Chinese traditions have to change or perish – such as the son entering the father's business, large and frequent family gatherings, and offspring living with and caring for aged parents.

The hectic pace of Hong Kong life is placing high stress on many of the upholders of these traditions. Emigration amongst the professional population in the last ten years has left upheavals in its wake. Often ageing parents are not willing to leave Hong Kong, or are prevented from following the younger generation by a host country's immigration restrictions. Demand in Hong Kong for nursing homes and homes for the old is increasing – whereas ten years ago it was unthinkable that Chinese sons and daughters would be putting their parents into an institution instead of caring for them at home. The general trend is painful for families to accept, and they are paying a price for this change.

Loyalty

Nevertheless, family loyalty and solidarity provide members with tremendous comfort and support. Whether it is to attain business objectives or to soothe feelings of personal discontent, family members generally rally round, regardless of rights and wrongs. Within the Hong Kong family structure, the adage 'blood is thicker than water' is to the point. The saying, 'keep the irrigation water within your own farmland' also depicts the idea of keeping the benefit within your own family. This idea is most clearly seen in marriage alliances that solidify various business connections; though the modern concept of marriage for love makes it harder for families to dictate conditions to their offspring.

The principle of loyalty applies also to the sovereign. In modern times, when there is no personal sovereign, it is represented by patriotism, or loyalty to the nation. This principle, *zhong*, is difficult to assess under present conditions in Hong Kong. Loyalty to this state is a recent concept. Twelve years ago, advocacy of rights and privileges for Hong Kong people as citizens was hardly thought of. Loyalty to the employer, on the other hand, is of long standing. The old system of a son succeeding the father in a secure job, flourishing a generation ago, is rarely followed now. The general impression given by the Hong Kong workforce today is of mobility. Emigration of professional and technical staff led to widespread local recruitment and promotion of their successors, which broke the tradition of 'a job for life'. Competition to hire the best available professional has accelerated careers of young skilled specialists. This process also created a strong and often haphazard flux of development, turning young and inexperienced professionals into executives. The shift of political loyalty away from London and towards Beijing is apparent among those who clearly pledge loyalty one way or the other, though fence-sitting is much in evidence.

Hierarchical Nature of Personal Relationships

Professional and social relationships in Hong Kong, like personal relationships, are vertical in nature. The order of a hierarchy of rank and authority is clearly reflected in rituals and manners. Simple examples include precedence for seating at dinner tables, or even who walks through a door first. The submissiveness of the Hong Kong people to those above them is well known. Therefore, insubordination would never be overt. Generally, when an underling disagrees with people in authority he expresses his dissent through discreet sabotage; never in open argument. This seeming acquiescence combined with back-stabbing, a mix of passive and aggressive behaviour, comes about through ingrained lack of the courage to speak out against the general custom and against particular authoritarian decisions of a father, boss, teacher, or husband. The Qing dynasty epic, *Dream of the Red Chamber*, and the twentieth century modern novel *Family*, read by Chinese school children despite prohibition by parents, give plenty of examples of surreptitious flouting of authority. These lessons reinforce the tradition that achievement is by stealth. Indeed, the novels make it extremely clear why the Chinese are such great politicians and strategists.

On less of an epic scale, we saw something of this in the Work and Leisure chapter. An employee will seem to accept an 'inappropriate' task, and not carry it out. This is something most readers will remember having practised, and having had practised against them. But note that they remember because in each case the step was exceptional, not habitual.

191

ESTABLISH YOUR GUANXI *BEFORE DEALING*

It is never quite *de rigueur* to confront any issue head on. Rather, it is important for you, the newcomer in the community, to invest time in finding out the *guanxi* between people. If you want to meet someone then find a third party, who has an established *guanxi*, to sow some seeds first. Be patient and wait for the opportune time. This process, although slow, will ensure that all parties concerned are ready to discuss the topic in question. The process might be described in Western social science terminology as 'managing expectations'. Use of third party mediation is common in Hong Kong. It is important to find the right party in terms of rank and status to represent your cause. Do not forget the invisible account, *maijiang*, when *guanxi* is used for giving or gaining face. There is no set formula. The procedure resembles an art that can only be perfected with practice; but before you begin to practise, you need awareness of your objectives and the route by which they might be achieved.

Trust

Next there is the issue of *xinyong,* trust. 'To earn your rights' is probably one of those concepts that the Hong Kong ethos takes for granted. The work ethic applies, no matter who you are or who your father is. Sometimes you hear that if you do not work hard in Hong Kong, there must be something wrong. There is so much work to be done in so little time, how can you be so lazy? This type of programming starts in the nursery school. Hardworking people are often perceived as more trustworthy, but hard work alone is not enough. The concept of *xinyong* in the Hong Kong context is not easy to define. It is essentially tied into past performance in that invisible record of accounts, and intertwined with the concept of face and relationships. Therefore, credentials are diligently striven for; material symbols of wealth are often ostentatiously displayed; names are dropped, and one is seen: at the right places and with the right people. These all become parts of the show – and unspoken commodities for trading in the unseen market, the pragmatic co-operation system. Grapevine gossip is the unofficial policing of these networks, that keeps in motion the approved version of the information flow. Criticism is easily earned. Support from the community depends greatly on the image that has been created in one's circle of influence. These right circles provide Hong Kong's only basic safety net.

Some local Chinese outsiders, though they understand the system, belong to no circle. They may go to great lengths to create an external image of belonging. Unfortunately, these images do not fool many pairs of eyes; and the hierarchical nature of society ruthlessly slots an imposter into his category of 'out' rather than 'in'.

The Inner Circle

Are you now ready to take the next flight out of Hong Kong? Well, don't. Obviously your experience will not be directed along such harsh lines. You will no doubt steer clear of entanglement with Triads and with family clans. You should just know that there are two impenetrable systems; one wholly evil, and the other with values independent of good and evil. Few if any of your Chinese contacts will be connected with organized crime. Most will be lightly or heavily involved with the family system, and all of them will always know better than you how it works. By no means all will be as calculating as we have suggested. It helps to have seen the worst, nevertheless.

This is one reason for the suggestions we offer at the end of this chapter: the idea that a local colleague or client could be (or seem) more Western than   Eastern – or, in another dimension, more traditional than modern. If you know what to look for, and note his conversational responses, you may be better able to approach him tactfully and to your mutual advantage. This, in turn, should ease your adjustment and help you to become engaged with rather than confused by Hong Kong.

WILLINGNESS TO TAKE RISKS

Hong Kong is full of people who live from day to day, with a penchant for taking risks. There is enormous interest and participation in Chance, and enormous profits are made through it – whether the medium is horse racing, cards, mahjong, the stock market, commodity trading, the big commercial deal or the thrill of leaving negotiation and bargaining and agreement to the last moment: 'pushing the envelope' as the Americans say. Some 'players' aim to create ultra-high-pressure as part of the fun, stimulating the adrenaline flow. For others the pressure is a by-product, hazardous to health. In either case it may become a vicious circle of addiction.

The networks and circles of influence are at times divided according to interest groups, rather like an inner ring at auctions, with different rules for different games. The price for newcomers of learning the hard way can be costly. And all the more so if a foreign newcomer chances his arm. One rule of thumb is, never enter into a big game unless you have the support of a big player. The strength of the informal structure makes it possible for those who grew up in the ethos to stay in the game and out-psych the competitors. Ultimately, the one with the most staying power is the one who is best placed to predict and manipulate the outcome.

It may be news to some that fortune-telling is based on number combinations and statistics. But it is intuition that makes one soothsayer, one gambler or one entrepreneur more successful than another.

Do not be frustrated if you do not get a precise answer to your questions at times. Think in terms of 'it could be looked at from this angle or that angle'. Accept 'it could be this ... or it could be that ...' as an interim answer.

The discrepancies between the formal and informal institutions will be the hardest elements of the culture for you to assess and negotiate. The more intangible aspects of a society, belonging to the realm of mental programming, manifest themselves through stories and folklore, heroes and superstars, rituals and ceremonies. As in many cultures, the grapevine reinforces versions of stories to mould the unspoken virtues. The well loved activity of eating around the table for hours is, in fact, an indoctrinating channel. Such activities are crucial for the programming of young minds. The patriarchs of the family will emphasize the current gossip and elucidate virtues and consequences. It is also a time for pledging loyalty to the clan, as there are inevitably factions within the system, so that expressions and intentions are made clear.

The distribution of power and authority manifests itself in Hong Kong's invisible bureaucracy as person-centred. That is to say, the informal structure of the culture will allow some back-door diplomacy. Obviously the British administration has created a strong formal bureaucratic system; however, in many of the more Chinese structures, the ultimate decisions are still made by the few in power. In terms of the variety of organizations – whether it is a marriage, a family or a business – the concept of delegation of power or responsibility is difficult to implement. The 'expert' in charge of a seminar or workshop understands that participants find more comfort in an authoritarian style than in a democratic atmosphere. Resistance will be strong if too many decisions are left to the members.

What about the willingness to take risks as against the ability to live with uncertainties? The balance on the tightrope is the ability to make a split-second decision whether the person taking the risk will feel that he will have to shoulder the blame if things go wrong. There is much avoidance of decisions when a person lower down the hierarchy feels that the only reward would be punishment if things go wrong. Adopting 'A' shaped shoulders, which means pushing the blame onto someone else, known as *lai* in Cantonese, is a practice that children pick up early at school. Another process is what is neatly called *verbal taichi*, a form of slow motion discussion which gracefully avoids responsibility without overtly saying so. Mastery of these skills is difficult for those who did not grow up here. However, spotting these practices in action is at worst entertaining, and at best enlightening. The duality – of money risk and procedural caution – is a continuous balancing act that tests and exercises the life skills of those who thrive in Hong Kong, and keeps them on their toes.

A MASCULINE AND COMPETITIVE SOCIETY

Hong Kong is very much a masculine society. One might say that no elaboration is necessary, because of its strong patrilineal-descent structure. Traditionally, female infants are not valued as highly as male. However, the concept of masculinity in Hong Kong can be expanded. It incorporates the meaning of 'big is beautiful', 'more is better', 'loud is stronger' and perhaps 'flashy is sexier'. These values seem to be diametrically opposed to some of the basic Chinese values of frugality, harmony within the group, respect for elders, and so on. Yet the competition that characterizes Hong Kong has mothers pushing their children to strive to be Number One in the class, and the young executive to be promoted before his peers; the impetus thus acquired and sustained prompts each industrialist to surge ahead of his rivals. These tendencies are the strength and foundation upon which the success of Hong Kong is based. The myths and stories of heroic entrepreneurs reinforce them. Yet the dynamic interactions between the basic Chinese values and these masculine traits must be confusing to the newcomer, if not, also, to the Hong Kong people themselves.

But neither those characteristics nor their combination is altogether strange. Consider football and other less artificial forms of tribal conflict. Participants know the rules. They are loyal to the captain or submissive to the chief, and helpful to team-mates or members of the clan. They direct their risk-taking and aggression outwards. In Hong Kong, as on the field of play, there may seem to be little scope for neutral behaviour towards people who are neither family/firm nor rivals/opponents. 'We' are Montagues and everyone else must therefore be a Capulet. Perhaps that overstatement is the right note on which to end this description of what is unusual – but by no means out-of-this-world – about the Chinese people of Hong Kong.

CONCLUSION

In this chapter we have made a point of describing systems of thought and behaviour that are deeply traditional and intensely Chinese. These two characteristics do not always go together. When they do, and when they are at their finest, the combination may be called Confucian. Alas, the good name of the Sage is tarnished by people who carelessly (or carefully) dignify anything of this kind as Confucian.

We have shown here and earlier that both the better and the worse aspects of the Chinese way of dealing are being weakened by education abroad and international practices in Hong Kong. We have also implied that, at their worst, these Eastern family networks resemble those which have spread from as far West as Sicily. You will recognize some of the local deceptions and disloyalties as an extended form of what makes fiction, and even life, in the West interesting and difficult. There is nothing wholly new under the Eastern sun.

So, what of the colleague or client with whom you are now lunching? Does he (or she) say rather little, from what seems to be a closed – not to say inscrutable – mind? Or is your friend being enthusiastically and convincingly more British than the English, or more American than the Yanks? Do not be deceived; but do not suppose that either of these acts is pure deception. The quiet luncher will understand you and your mental processes more than you his. The performance of the voluble chap is both a compliment to you and a piece of self-indulgence. However little the influence of tradition on him, though, he will still be more Chinese-minded than Western.

As he enjoys his roast lamb and roast potatoes, ask him what he eats at home. Ask him (or her) about celebrating Christmas, and the Lunar New Year. Enquire how he spends his annual holidays, and with how many companions. You will do this as a combination of social chat and sympathetic interest in his variant of the Hong Kong way of life. It may help you to assess the extent to which he is equally 'at home' in his two cultures. He meanwhile will be taking a view of where you stand on the traditionalist-progressive (or conservative-liberal or formal-bohemian) spectrum. That is a game we can all play. Everyone inclines to one or other of those two sides. So don't forget to adjust your first assessment of him when you have decided whether he is more, or less, old-fashioned than you are.

CULTURAL QUIZ

Now that you have read the chapters on Hong Kong, have acquired a good deal of factual information, and are aware of some of the unique characteristics of its society and its people, you must think that you are ready to face all types of situation that living in Hong Kong can produce. This quiz gives you an opportunity to test how you would fare in various predicaments. Some of the scenarios are normal; you will meet them often while you live here. Others have been invented and may seem to you somewhat contrived. Laugh and wail in disbelief if you will – but these situations are based on actual occurrences. Remember, when you find yourself perplexed: keep your cool. Also remember that patience is a virtue, and will receive its just rewards. The Chinese character, *ren* – literally 'to endure' (you will see it everywhere) – suggests a good philosophy to emulate.

SITUATION ONE

You have invited a few Hong Kong Chinese friends to your home to dinner. Each has brought you a present, intriguingly wrapped in a parcel tied with a ribbon. Should you:

A   Open the packages immediately in front of all the guests, praising each gift in elaborate language, and announcing how much you love it;

B   Thank the givers graciously and sweetly, and put the presents aside;

C   Hand all the presents back to the givers and insist that they take them home?

Comments

Option *B* is your only choice. It is out of the question for you to reject a gift that has been brought into your home. If it is really so valuable as to constitute an embarrassment as well as a bribe, you can settle the score the next day. Opening a present in front of everybody could humiliate the giver who might fear, regardless what pleasant noises you make, that you dislike the gift. And he would lose face if he thought his present modest in comparison with what the others had brought. Furthermore, the gift is for you to savour, not for everybody else present to ogle. Gift giving is a personal matter, and the Hong Kong people are a suspicious lot. You do not want to provide the others with an opportunity to gossip about the motives of the giver. If the gift is too lavish, they may say that he is bribing you to gain an advantage; if the gift is too small, they may say the giver is miserly.

Multiply this potential havoc by the number of guests bearing gifts, and settle with relief for option *B*. However, when a gift is obviously a box of candies or a bottle of wine, it would be nice to open it to share with all your guests. But there may be more than one box of candies; or you may already have prepared the drinks for the evening – and plan to recycle any consumable gifts. ... So it is up to you whether you open any of those. This is your decision, not a cultural one. If the chocolates are green from mould – and not because they are mint covered – you put them aside and say nothing. Recycling hostess gifts is such a common practice, and you do not want to embarrass the person who brought you the sweets. If you know her well, you can tell her about the green chocolates and you can share a good laugh. One of the leading chocolate importers in Hong Kong has been known to keep merchandise on the shelves a little too long.

Incidentally, unless it is a very large party, invitations in Hong Kong are initially given over the telephone. Invitations to dine at home always include spouses. The hostess will telephone your guests unless she has not met them, in which case the host will. Having secretaries telephone personal invitations to dine is arrogant and impolite. Of course if you and your wife are out of town when the party is being set up, your secretary will have to do the telephoning: always to the guest's secretary – if there is one. Always send a reminder near the date of the dinner. You can send an invitation card, or remind your guests by telephone or fax. This gesture shows that you are sincere in wanting your guests to come.

SITUATION TWO

You are invited by a friend or colleague to dinner. The invitation card, or the hostess over the telephone, indicates that dress will be informal. Should you:

201

A Show up in blue jeans and a silk shirt;
B Appear in a coat and tie, with your wife in a nice dress;
C Present yourself in a dinner jacket with a black bow tie?

Comments

B is your choice. Actually, unless your host and hostess are particular about the outward appearance of their guests, it does not matter what you wear. *Informal* in Hong Kong, however, means coat and tie. It does not have to be matching coat and trousers, which is known as *lounge suit*. If your hostess wished you to appear in your best suit and your wife in her most elegant outfit, to go with her sterling silver and best table linen, she would have said *lounge suit*. If she wishes you to appear in casual attire, she will say *casual*, which is not the same as *informal*.

Do not let what you ought to wear worry you: no one except the most insecure host and hostess cares what you will wear. It is you they want to see, not the clothes on your back. Once, a birthday party was given for a young woman who was reaching the age of thirty. It was to be an outdoor barbecue at the height of Hong Kong's summer heat. The site of the festivities was a colonial-style house at Repulse Bay, which was soon to be demolished for redevelopment; so the people organizing the party thought that it would be a shame not to have a grand send-off for the house as well. The invitation said *Gulf Attire*, which meant black tie but without the dinner jacket, as is the custom in the Persian Gulf where the weather is perpetually hot. People showed up in black tie with and without the jacket, or in shorts as if they were going to play *golf*. A grand time was had by all. It did not matter what they wore. On the other hand you, as a newcomer, should probably pay attention to what the invitation card says and dress accordingly.

SITUATION THREE

This situation would not arise had the lunch taken place at your club;

but you asked a Hong Kong Chinese business associate to lunch in a restaurant. It was a wonderful lunch and both of you enjoyed the food as well as the conversation. As the waiter presents the bill, your business associate starts to grab it. Should you:

A   Let him pay the bill;
B   Start fighting him tooth and nail for the bill;
C   Say: 'This time please let me take care of the bill, because I asked you; you can be the host next time'?

Comments

The correct answer is option *C*. Your guest knows that you are the host, responsible for picking up the tab. On the other hand, for a Chinese it is the culturally correct thing to do to make a gesture to grab the bill. It will make you uncomfortable to fight for the bill because in your culture one does not offer to pay the bill if somebody else did the inviting, but you still must not let him pay since it is you who initiated the lunch meeting. The few words you will say, as in option *C*, will stop his efforts at grabbing the bill. The waiter understands because it is part of the ritual of dining in a restaurant. Under no circumstance should you suggest a Dutch Treat.

   Incidentally, there is a ten per cent service charge in almost all the restaurants you will patronize in Hong Kong. But an additional tip would be nice, especially if you have had good service from the waiter, or if you eat in the restaurant often. In the latter case, a *laisee* packet to the captain and your usual waiter during the Lunar New Year season will reap untold rewards during the ensuing year. It never hurts to say thank you with a tip after a good meal.

SITUATION FOUR

You have decided to invite a few ladies to lunch on a particular day. You make out a list and start calling the guests. Geronima Li or Simonella Beowolf, for instance, wants to know who else is coming before she even accepts or declines your invitation. Should you:

A   Give her the full list;

B   Say that it is none of her business whom else you are inviting, and bang down the telephone;

C   Mumble something to the effect that you are not yet certain who is coming because Geronima or Simonella is the first person you have called?

Comments

You resent having to reveal your guest list so you will not choose option *A* even under torture. Geronima or Simonella, of course, is committing a *faux pas*. By demanding to know the names of the guests, she sounds as if she really would rather not come to your luncheon unless your other guests were worthwhile to her. As you may not indulge yourself with *B*, option *C* is your only choice.

A word of warning, however. Since you are handling such an insensitive person as Geronima or Simonella, she will not receive your implied message and will probably continue to probe. Now you must weigh all considerations. Do you need to know this woman for any particular reason? If so, you will have to bend backwards to be pleasant to her. This may not be a cultural issue, and similar situations may occur outside Hong Kong. It is just that there are so many women's lunches here (known as the *taitai* lunches). Household help is available, so women can afford the time to enjoy lunches away from home. Remember, there is no free lunch. You may therefore not want to become a part of the *taitai* luncheon circuit, but it may be essential for you to accept and give such luncheon invitations – for a variety of reasons which amount to building up *guanxi*.

Therefore, you will need to cultivate or tolerate Geronima or Simonella. Remember, keep cool.

SITUATION FIVE

You have been invited to dinner in a Chinese restaurant, but you have not been told that you are the guest of honour. When you arrive, your host asks you to sit in the seat of honour, at the head of the table, the seat facing the door. Should you:

A Sit down as the host directs;
B Make some noises in declining the honour for a few moments, then sit where the host directs;
C Sit somewhere below the salt, and refuse to budge?

Comments

B is the correct choice. If you were not the guest of honour, your host would probably not have asked you to take the honoured seat. Choosing option *A*, however, would show a lack of humility besides taking it for granted that you should be more important than anybody else at this occasion.

If the entertaining takes place in a private dining room of the restaurant, this situation will not occur because guests are seated away from the table until all have arrived. Your host, then, will seat the guests of honour first. Even so, demurring does not hurt.

SITUATION SIX

A number of people are waiting for taxis, when you join the merry throng. Should you:

A Stay around and fight to be the first at the taxi door when it stops to discharge a passenger;

B Walk further towards the direction from whence come the taxis, so that you will be the first to hail an empty taxi should one approach;

C Organize a taxi queue on the spot?

Comments

Everybody takes option *A* or *B*. However, option *C* shows signs of gaining ground. In fact, several regular taxi queues were started in this manner by some enterprising soul or other waiting in a non-queue. The institutionalized queues in front of the YWCA in Macdonnell Road, at the back of the Bank of America Tower in Central, and in

front of the entrance of M at the Fringe by the Foreign Correspondents' Club, for instance, were all started in this way. You can bet,
however, that the individuals who started those queues were not Hong
Kong Chinese.

In general, the culture of Hong Kong does not include fair play,
nor showing politeness to strangers. Competition is so intense in
every aspect of life that if you can improve your chances of getting a
taxi by lessening those of your competitors, you will: perhaps by
walking higher and higher on the one-way Wyndham Street, facing
the coming traffic, so that you can catch an empty cab coming down
before it reaches the other hopeful passengers. You can be certain,
though, that someone else will walk higher than you. While the days
of being pushed aside as you enter a taxi seem, happily, to be almost over
competitors still try very hard to get to the taxi door in front of you.

SITUATION SEVEN

You have just arrived at your destination by taxi. The driver has been
playing his radio loudly, and paying no attention to your comfort as
he slammed on the brakes and increased speed each time he turned a
corner. The meter shows nineteen fifty. You give him two ten-dollar
bills and he does not hand you the fifty cents change. Should you:

A Forget the fifty cents and disembark;

B Stay put like the Rock of Gibraltar and demand the change that is due to you;

C Say pointedly 'keep the change', get out of the taxi and leave the door open?

Comments

Regardless of your understandable feeling that you are being taken for another ride, forget the fifty cents. A tip of less than three per cent of the fare is not generous by any yardstick. So you take option *A*, and perhaps add a couple of dollars too. You will find the driver visibly grateful. He may not thank you aloud, but he will open the door for you since the passenger doors are linked to his foot by a mechanical device; and he will not drive away while you are still half in the vehicle.

Demanding your change may satisfy your sense of fair play, but it is just adding fire to an already aggravating situation. The amount is not worth the hassle. For the reason indicated, you are not going to inconvenience the driver by leaving the door open. Remember, passengers are a challenge to the drivers, too.

In many instances, however, the driver may decide to keep an extra dollar or two as a tip without your consent. You are, then, justified in asking him to give you the correct change – radio or no radio. And that brings us back to unwritten options *D* and *E*. If the radio makes your head hurt, say you have a headache and ask for mercy; and carry enough in small denominations to pay what you want to pay.

SITUATION EIGHT

You are eating out in a restaurant with a few friends, and the waiter is unhelpful. He appears to be uncivil, and service is slow. You have ordered the meal to be served family-style, but there is a long wait between courses. You have ordered a dish with a delicious gravy but the rice just is not coming. On top of it all, the noise level in the restaurant is intolerable, and your temper is rising. Should you:

A   Walk out in a huff leaving the meal unfinished and refusing to pay the bill;

B   Call the manager and ask him to remove the waiter;

C   Appeal to the waiter's better nature and ask him to hurry up the service?

Comments

There is no clear choice but option A is to be adopted only under severe provocation by the waiter's behaviour and manner. By refusing to pay the bill, especially if you have already consumed a couple of dishes, you would cause a great deal of commotion. There would be an unpleasant scene as you were leaving the restaurant, ruining your evening still further. You could modify option A by offering to pay for what you have already eaten, and cancel the rest of the dinner.

Option C is the least undesirable, taking a long view, because it will involve your meeting the waiter halfway. You may not want to lower yourself to plead for service, especially since you feel that what you want is your right and not a favour to be dispensed at the waiter's pleasure. However, by appealing to his sense of fair play you give him face, and he will be on your side in whatever battle there might be in the kitchen, to get your food served in the shortest time span he can muster. Ideally you negotiate for a hot delicious-dish replacement to come with the eventual hot rice.

Option *B* is possible, and probably the most effective way to get your food on the table. However, you do not know the reason behind the slow serving. The bottleneck may be in the kitchen, upstream of the dining room service. If you succeed in having the waiter removed, you cause him to lose face in front of a restaurant full of people; you might cause him to lose his job as well.

SITUATION NINE

You are in a shop which stocks the item you have been searching for all over town. The sales assistant is unhelpful. She is surly and refuses to bring out more of the same item, so that you may choose from a wider selection. Should you:

A   Walk out in a huff without buying what you want;
B   Ask to see the manager and have her wait on you herself;
C   Swallow your pride and buy the item even though you are not happy with the colour or the quality?

Comments

In this case, adopting option *C* is not intelligent, unless you feel that the price justifies such a compromise. If you are reasonably sure that by looking through more items you will be able to get what you want, by all means adopt option *B*.

The logical thing, in this competitive world, is to adopt option *A*. You will have to look elsewhere for the particular item of merchandise, but you will feel a lot better.

SITUATION TEN

You have been invited to meet the grandmother of a Chinese friend or associate for the first time. The old lady likes you. Despite the language gap, she has decided to make conversation. During the conversation, she asks for your age, why you are not yet married or, if you are, why you have no children yet. Then the conversation progresses inevitably to the amount of your salary. Should you:

A Tell her to mind her own business and stop being so nosy;
B Ask her to guess the answers to all her questions;
C Ignore her questions and talk about something else instead?

Comments

It depends on how you feel. Obviously you cannot be so rude as to take option A. Your friend, if he is sensitive at all, should have come to your rescue before this routine gets so far. Your friend should say something like, 'Ah, Granny, foreigners do not like to be asked these questions!' But perhaps he is reluctant to dictate his grandmother's behaviour, and you are left to cope.

A compromise option C is possible, for you are not unwilling to tell her your age, and say something completely nonsensical in answer to the other questions, by way of humouring the old lady. Remember, the Chinese do not like to say no, so she will understand that you are trying to evade her questions by changing the subject and talking about something else. The most polite option to choose, however, is option *B*. It will prolong the conversation, and lessen the awkwardness between you; there is no need for you to confirm or deny her conjectures.

SITUATION ELEVEN

You are an Australian woman travelling by yourself on the MTR. A well-dressed Chinese man of indeterminate age comes up to you and compliments you on your hair. Then he announces to the entire train that you smell like cow dung. Should you:

A   Slap his face and tell him that he is unspeakably rude;
B   Ignore him and find another place in the train to stand;
C   Stay put; but, looking at your fellow passengers, twirl your index finger while pointing it to your temple, indicating that the man is crazy?

Comments

As soon as he has commented on your hair, which is a personal remark one does not make to strangers in any culture, you should find some way to distance yourself from him, which is a pre-emptive option *B*. Option *A* is not to be adopted under any circumstance. Neither is option *C*. Obviously the man is at least a little touched when he makes such an insulting remark aloud. By provoking him in choosing option *A* or option *C*, you only make matters worse. As it is, fellow passengers who understood his remark are already embarrassed at him. Those who do not speak English will be interested only if you react.

SITUATION TWELVE

One of Hong Kong's senior men-about-town is sitting next to you at a formal dinner. He asks audibly whether you would mind him lighting a cigar. Since, in your opinion, such an act would emit both smoke and aroma that not everybody would find pleasant, you reply in a dulcet but audible voice that yes, you would indeed mind. He lights up just the same. Should you:

A   Tell him that you did say you would mind;
B   Smile pleasantly and say nothing;
C   Go to the ladies' room to cool off?

Comments

Yes, the man is rude and insensitive to ignore the clear wish of a neighbour, especially since he asked whether you would mind. Obviously he was not expecting a negative answer to what he considers a routine question, and thinks that the answer ought to have been an automatic 'Of course not, please go ahead'. Your frank response has made him lose face in front of the entire table of ten other persons. In this defiant gesture of lighting up his cigar, he clearly demonstrates to himself that there is no need to accept dictation from a woman.

What would have been the culturally correct response from you? Perhaps, had you merely smiled and made an inconspicuous gesture with your chin, you would have conveyed the message that it was not a good idea to smoke a cigar at a public gathering. Had your husband been this man's boss, or had he wanted something from your husband very badly, he would have heeded your understated wish; but not otherwise. This is a no-win situation. Go to the ladies' room to cool off and avoid smoke; or grin and bear it.

SITUATION THIRTEEN

You have decided to buy a basket of fruit to take to a friend, and have chosen a posh gift shoppe instead of using the van which carries fruit and vegetables to your building twice a week. You buy three mangoes at twenty dollars each, six peaches at ten each, two nectarines at fifteen each, six oranges at five each, and a bunch of bananas at twenty dollars. The basket is fifteen dollars. You hand him a five hundred dollar bill and wait for your change. Now, you are mathematically gifted and have been trained to add in your head without a calculator. So, when you hear the vendor say 'that will be three hundred and forty dollars', you know that he is trying to cheat you. Should you:

214

A Tell him that he is a cheat, demand the return of your five hundred dollars and walk out;

B Pay the amount he asked without murmur;

C Tell him that his total is incorrect and add together with him until you reach the correct number?

Comments

It is doubtful whether option *A* is an option at all, because the vendor will never return the money no matter what names you bring to bear. If his skin is thick enough to want to cheat you, for certainly that is his intention, he is not going to be shamed into giving back your money. Never give any merchant your money until you have agreed upon the price.

Option *B* is not an option either, because it is not the correct amount. Therefore, you are left with option *C*. It is troublesome, but you must spend as much time as it takes, while controlling your temper, so that you pay the right amount, and not one dollar more.

SITUATION FOURTEEN

You are with a group of Hong Kong natives and you are discussing all kinds of subject, from money and politics to personal matters. You have told them all about your family, your father and mother – where and when they were born, where they went to school, how they earn their living – and even about your grandparents. Suddenly you notice that one of your friends has said nothing about his parents. Should you:

A Probe – with specific questions about the friend's parents and their pedigree;

B Announce that you are not going to say anything more about your family unless he returns the compliment;

C Change the subject of conversation?

Comments

Options *A* and *B* are not tactful. Hong Kong family relationships are complicated. For one reason or another, your friend may wish to hide his ancestry. His parents might not be educated, which would not bother you but could upset him – especially if you have described your parents' illustrious degrees. Perhaps his father holds a menial job; or his mother may be a concubine and your friend is ashamed of the relationship. So, choose option *C*. If you are really good friends, he will reveal all in time – when he is sure you will not despise him because of his family background.

SITUATION FIFTEEN

You are walking your silent Yorkshire Terriers on Bowen Road and a family of father, mother and children come from the other direction. The father barks 'Wow! Wow! Wow!' at your dogs, and your dogs go berserk. The children are visibly frightened. The father goes 'Tsk, tsk' tsk! Bad dogs!' Should you:

A Tell the father that he is an imbecile;
B Shorten the leashes and pull the dogs closer to you;
C Say something soothing to the children while glaring at the father?

Comments

Option *A* is based on a true premise, for no sane person would go out of his way to tease a strange animal, but it is not the right time or place to educate a grown man. You should have begun option *B* as soon as you saw the family approaching, in any case; and now you must say in your gentlest tone something to calm the children.

Hong Kong children have been taught to be afraid of animals, especially dogs, since dogs are viewed as guards rather than pets. In this case, where the father has behaved so immaturely, it is up to you to assure the children that your dogs are harmless.

SITUATION SIXTEEN

You ring a business associate or a friend, in his office, and somebody answers the telephone. You ask for the person by name. The voice answers 'Mr Lee hasn't come back yet.' Should you:
A Assume that Mr Lee has come into the office already but has gone out temporarily;
B Leave a message for him to return your call, thank the voice, and hang up;
C Pursue further the whereabouts of Mr Lee?

Comments

The phrase 'hasn't come back yet' can have a host of meanings. It could mean that Mr Lee has not yet come to the office today, or that he will be out of town for the rest of the week. Under no circumstances should you choose option *B*; you must ask more questions to find out when you can expect a call from your friend. Option *A* is almost never justified because it usually means that Mr Lee has not so far come into the office.

217

Option *C* is your best choice. Unless you keep on asking questions, you are not going to find out the whereabouts of the person you want or when you can communicate with him. Our favourite answer to this sort of probing is 'Mr Yang hasn't come back yet. He is in the toilet.'

ISSUES OF CONCERN

As 1997 draws closer, people of Hong Kong speak with confidence, at least in public, about looking forward to the days after 30 June 1997 when Hong Kong becomes a Special Administrative Zone of the People's Republic of China, and when the policy of *One Country – Two Systems* will become actuality. Several thinking men and women, not a part of that chorus, have been asked to make a list of what they see to be the major issues of concern for the decade of the 1990s. These men and women work in the fields of brokerage, counselling, education, fund-raising for non-profit organizations, fund management, household management, investment banking, journalism, law, property sales and management, radio broadcasting, wholesale trade and retail trade.

AREAS OF CONCERN

Their areas of concern are presented here in alphabetical order, each with a brief description, in the person's own words as much as possible. There are more items than respondents, because no attempt has been made to eliminate any of the issues mentioned by the people asked, and because they have many concerns. One or two issues were given tongue in cheek; since they are of interest to the people of Hong Kong, they have been included in our list. We have exercised no value judgement and have excised no topic.

Autonomy

Hong Kong must have its own government chosen by the people, and should enjoy autonomy even after it becomes a part of the People's Republic of China. The most opportune time to attain this status is through political reforms to be completed two years before 30 June 1997, when the next general election of Members of the Legislative Council takes place in 1995.

Being Gaped at on the MTR

Expatriates in Hong Kong – those without car and driver as their perquisites, at least – commute by public transport. Ordinarily, fellow commuters have paid little attention. Increasingly, these expatriate commuters notice that they are being stared at overtly by fellow passengers. They are also disturbed by occasional rude remarks uttered aloud.

Brain Drain

With the emigration of Hong Kong's professional and executive talents, the need to import expatriate workers is making it expensive to run a business. When private companies, and the Government as well, sponsor the training of local personnel, they lose these persons within a short time afterwards to better opportunities. Despite much publicity on localization of civil service jobs, the Agriculture and

Fisheries Department, for instance, still hires vets from overseas on expatriate terms because local veterinarians, including some trained at Government expense, prefer private practice.

Chemical Abuse

Children and teenagers getting involved with drugs and alcohol are not confined to expatriate families. Chemical abuse is becoming a problem for Chinese families in Hong Kong as well, as traditional family structure weakens. Drugs are available. It is also easy to obtain alcoholic drinks.

Civil Service

The civil servants are taking fewer initiatives and are becoming passive due to greater politicization as well as the China factor. Decision-making, as a result, is becoming even slower. As experienced expatriate civil servants leave, there is juggling for power among the local staff leading to decision-making that may not be in the public interest.

Corruption

The most obvious abuses through corruption in the public and private sectors have been obliterated through the establishment of the Independent Commission on Crime in Hong Kong. Meanwhile, the ICAC is being accused of disregarding the civil rights of individuals. Corruption from across the border, as well as that in resurgence locally, is also affecting behaviour in Hong Kong.

Domestic Abuse

As Hong Kong becomes increasingly unsettled and its society more complex, domestic abuse of women and children is on the rise. Abuse of domestic workers who live with their employers is the more worrying when the Immigration and Labour Departments do not seem to be able to produce adequate laws for the protection of domestic helpers in Hong Kong. Abuse of expatriate wives by expatriate husbands is beginning to attract media attention.

Education

The education system needs an extensive overhaul, but even reformers cannot agree on premises and strategy. Instead of rote learning, the young men and women of Hong Kong should be trained to think for themselves, to draw a conclusion only after they have examined the facts, and to be prepared to take on individual, political and social responsibilities. New and better programmes for training teachers need to be adopted. The workload of the teachers should be reassessed. Instead of spending every hour in the classroom or correcting exercises, teachers should be given more time in which to prepare lessons that fit each individual class, and counsel children who need adult guidance.

Environment and Conservation

The air, land and water pollution in Hong Kong must not continue, and conservation of the environment should become a top priority of the Government as well as of individuals. For the moment, there seems to be little community or individual effort to eliminate pollution, to keep the environment clean, to reduce waste or to recycle materials.

Equality and Human Rights

Although much improved since during the decade of the 1980s, there is still a large discrepancy between rewards enjoyed by men and women. Wages are higher for men; job advertisements still require photographs and personal information such as age and gender. The proposal to establish a Human Rights Commission is not receiving support from either the Hong Kong or the Chinese authorities.

Fear of Chinese Interference

The fear of Chinese interference after 1997, despite the fifty-year pledge, is making it difficult for people to make business decisions.

Handicapped Children and Adults

Hong Kong boasts an excellent social welfare programme providing care and training for handicapped children. Efforts must be made to see that these programmes continue and are extended to include parents of the handicapped as well as handicapped and elderly adults.

Horse Racing

Horse racing must continue as it is one of the most important traditions of Hong Kong. How else would people spend Saturday afternoons and how else would charities be funded?

Inflation and Rising Costs

Rising costs, especially in rents, are making Hong Kong one of the most expensive places in the world. Companies and individuals are reluctant to adopt long-term strategy or make long-term investments here. Government has been seen to work hand in hand with property developers.

Internationalism

It is important to maintain Hong Kong's position as an international centre of business and finance. Its law and order, infrastructure, language abilities, and freedom must be maintained beyond 1997.

Investment

Hong Kong must maintain a functioning market for international investments and improve it constantly to be on par with other investment and financial centres of the world. Recognition must be given to Hong Kong as the most credible market China will have for a long time to come.

Language Skills

For Hong Kong to continue as a centre of international business and finance, the quality of the command of English must be elevated. The same rule can be applied to the quality of Chinese in Hong Kong. Deterioration in language training, for instance, has made the Hong Kong populace unable to cope in either Chinese or English. Adult education programmes should be adopted to improve language command in both English and Chinese. The media also must assume responsibility in not allowing the language command to deteriorate any further.

Law

Translation and application of common law and the existing body of laws, precedents, rules, and regulations into the Chinese language is essential. It must be in a manner that can be understood by those Chinese who do not have a command of the English language or legal traditions.

Law and Order

There is noticeable deterioration in law and order as a result of morale problems – and of a disintegration of the sense of unity and identity – among the police, the civil service, and the community. People are showing signs of becoming more militant and selfish. Robberies featuring imported felons and firearms are becoming more commonplace.

Materialism

Hong Kong is developing into a be-all and end-all materialist society at the expense of traditional standards of ethics, morals and values. Thought must be given as to how to introduce at least some of the Eastern and Western values to Hong Kong.

Money
Conditions for making money in Hong Kong must continue.

Nationality
The nationality issue will involve more than the ethnic Chinese of Hong Kong adopting Chinese nationality. Will they, individually or as a whole, have any protection against deprivation of their civil rights? What will happen to the ethnic non-Chinese who have been living in Hong Kong for several generations and have no other nationality?

PLA
What will be the role of the People's Liberation Army? It is known for certain that there will be a presence of uniformed Chinese armed forces in Hong Kong after 1997. Whereas the British military have been functioning largely outside the public purview, would the PLA be visible? Will they interfere with police matters?

Polarization and Division
Polarization and division of groups in Hong Kong resulting from realignment of allegiances during the transitional period between London and Beijing are affecting the private sector as well as the civil service.

Police
As an increasing number of members of the police force emigrate, will law and order deteriorate?

Putonghua
Will Putonghua replace Cantonese as the language of Government and the courts? Will all schools be forced to abandon instruction in Cantonese and change to Putonghua?

225

Rudeness

Shop assistants are increasingly rude to expatriates. Lack of response from Government officials to complaints from the public on lack of service and disturbance to their well-being – be it construction noise or the cheating taxi driver – is also noted.

Simplified Characters

Hong Kong and Taiwan are the only predominantly Chinese speaking places which still use the traditional characters. If the Chinese authorities should enforce simplified characters in Hong Kong, they will meet a great deal of resistance. Shall the Hong Kong will in this matter prevail?

Sino-Hong Kong Relationship

How can the relationship between Hong Kong and Beijing be handled with sensitivity without Hong Kong losing its rights and position as a centre of international economy?

Social Conscience

The development of a public social conscience should be nurtured.

The Stock Market

The volatility of the Hong Kong Stock Exchange cannot be blamed on vagaries of Hong Kong investors alone, since Hong Kong shares are attracting investments from abroad. Asia, especially Hong Kong, is viewed by global investors as the area of growth.

Television Standards on English-Language Channels

This is a serious problem since it is not only the quality of English that is abysmal. The choice of programmes is not overly intelligent either. The much touted satellite television is a disappointment. Hopefully, cable television being installed will take account of the interests of the audience in their choice of programmes.

Travel Documents

The decreasing acknowledgement of Hong Kong travel documents internationally is resulting in more visa requirements, thereby making it confusing and difficult for persons holding such documents to travel outside Hong Kong. If freedom of travel is to be included as a fundamental right of the Hong Kong people during the decade and beyond, their travel documents must be universally accepted.

COMMENT

It is interesting but not surprising to note that, although relationships with China appear as a concern on several individuals' responses, the future relationship between Great Britain and Hong Kong has not been mentioned.

The omission of certain other items may be thought revealing; for example, public transport and traffic congestion. Since everyone must go by public or private vehicle, from one place to another, these items should be of interest. It is true that newcomers usually marvel at the high quality and low cost of public travel in Hong Kong. It is only when they have been here for a while that they begin to complain.

IMPORTANT ISSUES –
SOUTH CHINA MORNING POST

Meanwhile, in early October 1993, on the eve of Governor Patten's second annual address to the Legislative Council, the *South China Morning Post* published the results of a poll on matters its readers would like to see the present Government act on. The following issues headed the list. They are presented with the percentage of respondents interested in each specific issue.

Law and order	56.9%
Sino-British relations	56.4%
Medical and health	51.4%
Housing	50.8%

Environment	48.8%
Education	48.6%
Corruption	47.6%
Social welfare	47.2%
Inflation	44.3%
Political reform	43.3%
Traffic	42.8%

BASIC FACT-FILE ON HONG KONG

AREA

1,070 square kilometres of land, 40% of which is made up of 21 country parks. The highest point is Tai Mo Shan (957 metres or 3,139 feet) in the New Territories.

The Four Major Districts

Hong Kong Island, Kowloon and New Kowloon, the New Territories, and the Outlying Islands.

POPULATION

6,019,900 at the end of 1993, according to Government statistics:

comprising 3,058,300 males and 2,961,600 females, with 21.7% on Hong Kong Island, 33.5% in Kowloon and New Kowloon, 44.5% in the New Territories and 0.3% on the Outlying Islands. The population density is 5,700 per square kilometre (26,180 in Hong Kong Island, Kowloon and New Kowloon; and 2,790 in the New Territories. The trend is towards the New Territories).

GOVERNMENT STRUCTURE

Governor – appointed by the Queen of the United Kingdom.

Civil Service – appointed by the Governor.

Executive Council – *ex officio* members and others appointed by the Governor.

Legislative Council – *ex officio* members and others appointed by the Governor; non-official members elected by functional constituencies, and directly elected by qualified voters in geographical constituencies.

Urban Council – appointed and elected members; responsible for urban services including sanitation, environment, recreation, libraries, sports.

Regional Council – appointed and elected members responsible for the New Territories; similar to Urban Council.

District Boards – appointed and elected members, plus New Territories rural committee chairmen and chairwomen to advise the Government on issues relating to districts.

Quasi government bodies – including the Hong Kong Trade Development Council, and the Hong Kong Tourist Association.

CURRENCY

The Hong Kong dollar is pegged to the US dollar at the rate of HK$ 7.80 = US$1.00.

HISTORICAL MILESTONES

1514	First Portuguese trading post at Tuen Mun
1841	British flag at Possession Point on Hong Kong Island
	Jardine, Matheson and Company godowns (warehouses) and counting houses to Hong Kong
1842	Free port status for Hong Kong
	Treaty of Nanking (Nanjing) ceding Hong Kong to Britain
1843	Treaty of the Bogue, Chinese allowed free access to Hong Kong for trade
	Sir Henry Pottinger, Governor of Hong Kong
1844	Sir John Davis, Governor of Hong Kong
1845	The *China Mail*, English-language newspaper

1846	The Hong Kong Club
1848	Sir Samuel George Bonham, Governor of Hong Kong
1849	St John's Cathedral
1854	Sir John Bowring, Governor of Hong Kong
1855	Last public execution in Hong Kong
1857	*Hong Kong Daily Express*
1858	Treaty of Tientsin (Tianjin) ceded promontory of Kowloon and Stonecutters Island to Britain; legalization of opium trade
1859	Sir Hercules Robinson (Lord Rosmead), Governor of Hong Kong
1861	Hong Kong and China Gas Company
	Hong Kong General Chamber of Commerce
	Botanical Gardens
1863	Issue of Hong Kong silver dollars
1864	Gas street lighting
1866	Sir Richard Graves Macdonnell, Governor of Hong Kong
1868	Tung Wah Hospital
1870	Telegraphic cable link to China: Hong Kong-Amoy (Xiamen)-Shanghai
1871	Hong Kong-Singapore cable link
1872	Sir Arthur Edward Kennedy, Governor of Hong Kong
1873	Missionary schools in Land Grant scheme
1877	Sir John Pope Hennessy, Governor of Hong Kong
	Ng Choy, first Chinese barrister admitted to Hong Kong bar
1879	Secular curriculum in Government and grant-in-aid schools
1880	Telegraphic link with the Philippines
	Ng Choy first Chinese non-official member of Legislative Council
1881	Government telephone system

1883	Sanitary Board, developed into Urban Council in 1936
	Hong Kong link to Shanghai and Foochow (Fuzhou) by cable
	Canton-Kowloon telegraph line
	Sir George Ferguson Bowen, Governor of Hong Kong
1884	Hong Kong Jockey Club
1887	The College of Medicine for the Chinese
	Sir George William Des Voeux, Governor of Hong Kong
1888	Peak Tram from the Cathedral to Victoria Gap
1889	Hong Kong Electric Company
1890	Public telephone system
1891	Sir William Robinson, Governor of Hong Kong
1896	Pedder's Wharf (Blake's Pier)
1898	Ninety-nine year lease of New Territories and New Kowloon
	Sir Henry Arthur Blake, Governor of Hong Kong
1900	Chinese General Chamber of Commerce
1902	Temple Ohel Leah
1903	China Light and Power
1904	Sir Matthew Nathan, Governor of Hong Kong
	Electric tramways on Hong Kong Island
	Reclamation project in Central
1907	Sir Frederick Lugard (Lord Lugard), Governor of Hong Kong
1910	Kowloon-Canton Railway
	Opium divans in Hong Kong and New Territories closed
1911	Revolution in China
	University of Hong Kong
1912	Republic of China
	Sir Francis Henry May, Governor of Hong Kong
1919	Sir Reginald Stubbs, Governor of Hong Kong

1923	Cenotaph
1925	Sir Cecil Clementi, Governor of Hong Kong
	Hong Kong seriously affected by labour unrest in Canton, lasting until 1926
1926	Sir Shouson Chou, first Chinese member of Executive Council
1928	Peninsula Hotel
1930	Sir William Peel, Governor of Hong Kong
1931	Anti-Japanese riots
1935	Sir Andrew Caldecott, Governor of Hong Kong
1936	Airmail service between Hong Kong and Britain
1937	Second Sino-Japanese War began in China (July)
	Sir Geoffrey Alexander Stafford Northcote, Governor of Hong Kong
1938	Sir Mark Aitchison Young, Governor of Hong Kong
	Canton fell to the Japanese, influx of 500,000 refugees to Hong Kong
1941	World War II, Japanese occupation of Hong Kong (December)
	Internment of civilians at Stanley, military at Argyle Street and Sham Shui Po POW Camps
1945	Liberation of Hong Kong from Japanese occupation (August)
1946	Return of British administration to Hong Kong – return of Sir Mark Young (see 1938)
	Roman Catholic Diocese
1947	Sir Alexander William George Herder Grantham, Governor of Hong Kong
1949	Communist victory in China, influx of refugees to Hong Kong
	First double-decker bus service
1950	Korean War
1951	UN embargo on trade with People's Republic of China

1953	Public housing scheme after squatter huts fire at Shek Kip Mei
1958	Sir Robert Brown Black, Governor of Hong Kong
	Completion of runway at Kaitak Airport
1960	Agreement with Guangdong provincial authorities to supply fresh water
1962	Influx of illegal immigrants from China
1963	Chinese University of Hong Kong
1964	Sir David Clive Crosbie Trench, Governor of Hong Kong
1965	Mrs Liu Shui-fu, first woman member of Legislative Council
1966	Lion Rock Tunnel
1967	Riots in Hong Kong
1969	Francis Chen-peng Hsu, first Chinese Roman Catholic Bishop of Hong Kong
1971	Social welfare scheme of public assistance
	Free primary education in government schools
	Sir Murray MacLehose (Lord MacLehose of Beoch), Governor of Hong Kong
1972	Hong Kong Arts Festival
	New Towns Programme
	Hong Kong Polytechnic
	Cross Harbour Tunnel (October)
1974	ICAC (Independent Commission Against Crime)
	Hong Kong Philharmonic Orchestra
1975	Hung Hom Railway Station (new terminus of the Canton to Kowloon Railway) opened by Queen Elizabeth II
1978	Vietnamese refugees began to arrive in boats
1979	Mass Transit Railway
1982	Sir Edward Youde, Governor of Hong Kong
	Sino-British negotiations on future of Hong Kong

	Vietnamese boat people confined to camps
	District Boards established
	China Light and Power Station at Castle Peak
1983	Formal Sino-British negotiations on Hong Kong began
	Linkage of Hong Kong dollar to US dollar @ HK$7.80 to US$1.00
1984	Government White Paper on Future Development of Representative Government in Hong Kong
	Margaret Thatcher, British Prime Minister, signed Sino-British Joint Declaration in Beijing and addressed Legislative and Executive Councils in Hong Kong
1985	Elections for 12 Legislative Councillors by functional constituencies
	Legislative Council to renovated Old Supreme Court Building
	Unified Stock Exchange at Exchange Square
1986	Daya Bay nuclear power station agreement signed
	Regional Council
	Death of Governor Sir Edward Youde in Beijing (December)
	Sir David Akers-Jones, Acting Governor of Hong Kong
1987	Sir David Clive Wilson (Lord Wilson of Tillyron), Governor of Hong Kong
1988	White Paper on 'The Development of Representative Government'
	Sir Ti Liang Yang, first Chinese Chief Justice
	Sino-British Joint Declaration on Hong Kong
	Permanent office of Sino-British Joint Liaison Group in Hong Kong
	Screening of Vietnamese boat people
1989	Mass rally of Hong Kong people after Tiananmen Square (June)

	British Government announcement that right of abode in the United Kingdom would not be granted to all Hong Kong residents
	Eastern Harbour Crossing Tunnel
	Open Learning Institute
	Massive Port and Airport Development Scheme
	Hong Kong Cultural Centre and Hong Kong Convention and Exhibition Centre
	British Government announcement of full British passports for a limited number in Hong Kong
1990	Basic Law of the Hong Kong Special Administrative Region (HKSAR) promulgated by the Chinese National People's Congress
	British-Hong Kong agreement to return non-refugee boat people to Vietnam
	Government announcement of finance to construct the Lantau Fixed Crossing leading to the new Chek Lap Kok airport
1991	Tate's Cairn Tunnel
	First direct election of 30% of Legislative Council
	Sale of first Government Bonds
	Memorandum of Understanding between Britain and China on the new airport signed
	Hong Kong Hospital Authority
	Teaching began at Hong Kong University of Science and Technology
1992	Christopher Francis Patten, Governor of Hong Kong
1993	Anson Chan, first woman and first local Chief Secretary of the Government of Hong Kong

PUBLIC HOLIDAYS

There are eleven statutory holidays each year, in addition to Sundays. Most of them fall on specific dates or days; others are shifted to Mondays. It is expected that after June 1997 holidays will be brought in line with those observed in the People's Republic of China. This would mean holidays of the British tradition, such as the Queen's Birthday, being eliminated and that May Day and the Chinese National Day might be added to the list which follows. Six of this longer list of public holidays are not statutory, which means that there is no legal obligation to give each employee the day off as a paid holiday.

Every Sunday
The first weekday in January
The day preceding Lunar New Year's Day
Lunar New Year's Day
The second day of the Lunar New Year
The third day of the Lunar New Year
Ching Ming Festival (grave visiting)
Good Friday
Easter Monday
Birthday of HM the Queen
The Monday following the Queen's Birthday
Tuen Ng Festival (Dragon Boat)
The Saturday preceding the last Monday in August
The last Monday in August (Liberation Day)
The day following the Chinese Mid-Autumn Festival
Chung Yeung Festival
Christmas Day
The first weekday after Christmas Day

FURTHER READING

Books on Hong Kong are available at local bookshops. They are instantly recognizable because almost all of them show 'Hong Kong' in their titles. Shop managers obligingly place them where they will catch your eye as you enter the door, or in a section clearly marked 'Local Interests' or 'Hong Kong'. The list which follows is by no means exhaustive, but I have selected the books I have found useful and enjoyable. It does not mean, however, that books I have left unmentioned are all humdrum. You will have to browse through the bookshops yourself to choose those you like.

Bilingual Street Guide

Before you even start to browse, however, you must buy at once the latest issue of *Hong Kong Streets and Places* by Hong Kong Government Publications. Even if you do not drive, you will need to consult a street map from time to time. This publication is more than a guidebook, it can be a lifesaver. The names of the streets are indexed in English and Chinese. If you point to the street you know by its English name, where it is listed in alphabetical order, a taxi driver, say, will be able to find its Chinese equivalent and take you to your desired destination.

Fiction

Most novels are undemanding, although physically they may be weighty. Several bestselling novelists have found Hong Kong a dramatic background for their work. As long as you do not confuse historical fiction with historical fact, novels can give you the flavour of a bygone era. Still in print are perennial favourites with more editions than can be counted on all your fingers and thumbs. James

Clavell's *Taipan*, taking place in the Opium War era with Canton, Macau and Hong Kong as background, is truly a good yarn with almost no glaring historical *faux pas*. The characters are strong and the ambience of early Hong Kong is convincing. A later novel that takes place during the 1960s, *Noble House*, with the typhoon and landslide as backdrop and boardroom battles as a major theme, disappoints; but it is readable nevertheless, since Clavell is such a master craftsman. *Dragon Tale* (1989) is an attempt by Leonard Rayner to bring Chinese players into the Hong Kong boardroom game.

My sister found at a church bazaar in Pittsburgh a charming and romantic novel on Hong Kong simply entitled *Hong Kong* (1958), published by Doubleday in New York; the action takes place in the time of the Opium War. The author, Mona Gardener, is a graduate of Stanford who had lived in Asia, including Malaysia, Japan and Hong Kong, during the 1950s. This book must be out of print, but I have placed my copy in the Library of the Royal Asiatic Society, now in the Urban Council Library at City Hall.

Robert Elegant's *Dynasty*, depicting Hong Kong's leading Eurasian family and its ups and downs, is pure fiction without any pretence of resembling what really happened; but a good aircraft or poolside companion, nevertheless. Richard Mason's *The World of Suzy Wong*, published by Fontana of Glasgow in 1959, racist and sexist though it is, and dated to boot, depicts the sentimental as well as the seamier side of old Hong Kong.

In a more literary direction, I have always found the writing of John Le Carré somewhat formidable, but have enjoyed thoroughly his *Honourable School Boy*, with recognizable but hybrid characters running in and out of the Foreign Correspondents' Club of an earlier period. A recent novel that takes places in Hong Kong is *Foreign Correspondents Club* by Anthony Spaeth (London, 1990).

Yesterday

There are many scholarly works on various aspects of Hong Kong's history – political, social, economic and so forth. Pre-eminently, you should consult *Research Materials for Hong Kong Studies* published by the Centre of Asian Studies, University of Hong Kong, with over three hundred resource pages – but only if you are writing a monograph of some sort on the territory. The best book from which to learn some of the history is *A History of Hong Kong* by Frank Welsh, just published in 1993 by HarperCollins in London. Despite its length of more than 600 pages, this is a highly entertaining book. Welsh, a merchant banker who used to live in Hong Kong, has conducted research meticulously and seriously, but has not allowed pomposity of historical personalities and decisions to stand in the way of his witty presentation of events.

Picture books on Hong Kong's past and present are legion. Some of them are exquisite and others merely commercial. You will just have to browse and pick out the ones you like for yourself. Two of my personal favourites are: *Hong Kong Heritage, A Personal View,* by Elyse Parkin (1979), with charming watercolours; and Alan Birch, *Hong Kong, the Colony That Never Was* (1991), with contemporary photographs. Two books published by Hong Kong's Form Asia – *Great Cities of the World Hong Kong* (1990) and *Above the Barren Rock, Spectacular Hong Kong From the Air* (1994) – are of high quality. *An Illustrated History of Hong Kong* (1991), by Nigel Cameron, is worthwhile for its historical photographs.

Today

Reading on a topic of current interest is *Hong Kong and China, For Better or For Worse*, by Frank Ching, author of *Ancestors*, published by the Foreign Policy Association in New York in 1985. The information in the book may be not up to date, but the succinct analysis of issues involved in the handing of Hong Kong to China in 1997 has remained valid. Subsequent events have proved Ching to be an astute observer of the China-Hong Kong scene. There is also *The End of Hong Kong* (1993) by Robert Cottrell, another astute observer of

China and Hong Kong. A more recent publication on this subject is Sir Percy Craddock's *My Experiences of China* (1994). Sir Percy was a member of the team that negotiated the agreement returning Hong Kong to Chinese rule in 1997.

Other books in this category include *The Future of Hong Kong, Towards 1997 and Beyond* (1987), edited by Hungdah Chu, Y C Jao, and Yuan-li Wu, and *Economic Future of Hong Kong* (1990) by Miron Mushkat. I recommend to you books on this subject written for an international readership primarily because, as a newcomer to Hong Kong, you will find them more user-friendly than local publications which take for granted familiarity with names, terms and events. You should also try to find *Hong Kong, Epilogue to An Empire* (1988) by Jan Morris.

To be brought wholly up to date with developments, you only need to open a newspaper or a journal – any of the three local newspapers and some of the overseas newspapers with international coverage – or any weekly journal such as *Far Eastern Economic Review* or *The Economist*.

If you work in the field of high technology and would like to find out how to translate your talent and knowledge into cash, then read *A Choice Fulfilled: the Business of High Technology* (1991), by Charles K Kao, the Vice Chancellor of the Chinese University of Hong Kong. He is renowned as the 'Father of Fiber Optics', the basis for our telecommunications revolution, and is an authority on such undertakings. Written with the interested general reading public in mind, this book traces the development of intricate technologies for practical use in the age of information.

The Good Old Days

Old-timers in Hong Kong have written about their experiences. Austin Coates, a graduate of Oxford and son of the composer Eric Coates, wrote *Myself a Mandarin, Memoirs of a Special Magistrate* (1968), reminiscences of his life as a colonial administrator in the

New Territories before villages were turned into new towns. It is written with compassion, a feeling of frustration, and a great sense of humour. Coates belongs to a generation which is literate as well as learned, and he is a master of the English language. If you read only one book on old Hong Kong, this should be your choice.

Anthony Lawrence, an octogenarian journalist retired from the BBC but from little else, has evidently traded his microphone for a typewriter. He has been most prolific on Hong Kong topics for two decades. Of his books, the one most interesting to readers here is *The Taipan Traders* (second edition 1992), commissioned to accompany a collection of beautifully reproduced China Coast School paintings of old Hong Kong. His latest, *The Fragrant Chinese* (1993) is full of knowledge, insight and wisdom. Lawrence is not sure whether any of his many Chinese friends are still speaking to him as a result of this publication, but you will find it entertaining and instructive. You will also find Colin Criswell's *The Taipans, Hong Kong's Merchant Princes* (1981) informative.

Meggie Keswick's *The Thistle and the Jade* (1982) was compiled to commemorate the 150th anniversary of the founding of Hong Kong's premier *hong*, Jardine Matheson, and Austin Coates wrote the delightful and informative *China Races* (1983) to commemorate the centenary of the Royal Hong Kong Jockey Club. *Foreign Mud* (1946) by Maurice Collins is a readable history of the Opium War written by a non-historian.

People and Customs

Hugh Baker's *Hong Kong Images, People and Animals* (1979) is so much in demand that it has been issued several times since as a paperback. Dr Baker informs and entertains readers interested in the Chinese tradition as practised in Hong Kong. Michael Harris Bond's *Beyond the Chinese Face, Insights from Psychology* (1991) is the 'all-time bestseller ever published by an academic press', in the words of its publisher. It is a scholarly work, intended for the general reader like you and me as well, a series of articles explaining what makes the Chinese what they are. Wang Gungwu's *The Chineseness of China* (1991) explores the theme of Chineseness in greater depth, from a historical perspective.

Turbans and Traders, Hong Kong's Indian Communities (1994) by Barbara-Sue White has just come onto the market, in time for you to learn more about some of the people of Hong Kong who are not ethnic Chinese.

Tales and insights within Government House can be found in a single book on the wives of successive governors of Hong Kong, *The Private Life of Old Hong Kong* (1991), by Susanna Hoe. At the other end of the social ladder, there is Maria Jaschok's *Concubines and Bondservants* (1988), a sociological study – but short and readable. These books should be on the essential reading list of all women and their men in Hong Kong.

The Moon Year by Juliet Bredon and Igor Mitrophanow, first published in 1927, was reprinted in Hong Kong in 1982. This is the fountainhead of all non-scholarly books on Chinese festivals, containing every bit of information you'll ever care to know about festivals and customs from one month to the next throughout the whole lunar year – ancestors, gods, beliefs, superstitions, dragon and lion dances, the lot; but it is a weighty undertaking, not to be digested at a sitting. A more portable work is *Chinese Festivals* (1982) by Joan Law and Barbara E Ward, which is confined to practices in Hong Kong.

Fauna and Flora

A revised and enlarged edition of Clive Viney's *Birds of Hong Kong* (1977), illustrated by Karen Phillips, will be in the bookshops by the time you read this page. It is comparable in utility with Roger Tory Peterson's guides to American birds. B M Walden and S Y Hu, *Wild Flowers of South China and Hong Kong*, two volumes (1977, 1987), will become constant companions on your walks through the country parks. Check with Government Publications near Star Ferry: there are other books on Hong Kong's fauna and flora, which include butterflies, fishes, and reptiles.

A Popular Guide to Chinese Vegetables (1982), text by Martha Dahlen and illustrations by Karen Phillips, has had several reprintings. Embracing Chinese cooking utensils and simple recipes, this book is more than a guide to vegetables. Armed with it, you will be well able to venture into the Chinese markets; and to put their food on your dinner table with aplomb. Further, you will gain a deep understanding of the vegetables as food items and as nature's works of art.

Out-of-the Ordinary Guidebooks to Interesting Places

There are many good books in this category, too, and in general guidebooks today are of high quality. You will just have to find for yourself the one you like best. Hong Kong Tourist Association publishes maps and little guide folders, mostly *gratis*, and you can have them for the asking in their office at the Kowloon side of the Star Ferry and in the basement of Jardine House.

Other publications include *Another Hong Kong, An Explorer's Guide* (1989), edited by Alan Moore, and Sally Rodwell's *A Visitor's Guide to Historic Hong Kong* (1991): wonderful books carefully researched and beautifully presented. You will want either or both in your library. The most portable though the most detailed book of this genre is *Historical Hong Kong Walks: Hong Kong Island* (1988) by a group of ladies led by the indefatigable Madeleine Tang. These women are curious to know all the details about everything they see, and so have provided you with factual and legendary answers to every question you can possibly have as you traipse along the routes of Hong Kong's historical past and its ever-changing present.

Complete Guide to Hong Kong Factory Bargains and *Hong Kong Restaurant Guide* seem to be constantly out of stock. They are in such demand that they are sold out almost before the shops can put them on the shelves. The American Chamber of Commerce issues *Living in Hong Kong*, a practical guidebook which is updated from time to time.

Satire, and Gentle Humour

The current guru of satire in Hong Kong is Nury Vittachi who is now penning the weekly 'Travellers' Tales' in *Far Eastern Economic Review*. His old columns from the *South China Morning Post* have been gathered in a single volume, *Only in Hong Kong* (1993). Political cartoons by Templar (Christopher Young) are also available in a single volume, *The Best of Basher* (1993). Larry Feign's 'The World of Lily Wong', the trials and foibles of a local woman married to a *gweilo*, appears daily on the second page of the *South China Morning Post,* and before long these cartoons will start your day as you pick up your first cup of coffee. If you miss a day or so it does not matter, because they are collected into single volumes and are published from time to time. While you are at the bookshops, also pick up Feign's *Aieeyaaaa*, which allows you glimpses into the Cantonese language in a hilarious way. To delve further into the mysteries of Chinese characters involving food and culture, look for *Swallowing Clouds* by A Zee. A Zee, according to the book jacket, 'was born in China, reared in Brazil, educated at Princeton and Harvard', and is a man.

COMMENT

By the time you finish these pages, and when you have browsed once through the shelves of the bookshops, you will have found books not on this list that are much more to your liking. Well done! Do not forget to browse through the libraries as well. Remember, in addition to the Urban Council libraries, any private club you are lucky enough to join will have its lending library; and all will have books on Hong Kong.

Happy browsing, and happy reading.

THE AUTHORS

Betty Wei is a research scholar. She is also much in demand as an informative and humorous speaker on topics concerning China and Hong Kong. Having lived for long in New York – and as a graduate of Bryn Mawr College, with a master's degree in international relations and a doctorate in modern Chinese history – Dr Wei has a unique understanding of both the Western and the Chinese traditions. A resident of Hong Kong since 1975, she has been a shrewd observer of its past and present economic, political and social changes.

Dr Wei is an honorary Lecturer in History at the University of Hong Kong. She is active in the community, serving on the boards of several educational and welfare organizations. Her publications include *Shanghai: Crucible of Modern China* (1987) and *Old Shanghai* (1993).

Elizabeth Li is a 'Change agent' in the fields of Organization Development and Strategic Management. She worked for over ten years in industry, before becoming a management consultant in 1986. She holds a Master of Science degree in organization development, from Peppardine University.

The focus of her present activity is on cultural differences within organizations. Three-quarters of her work relates to the absorption of Western concepts within the People's Republic of China. She is bicultural; for she was born in Hong Kong, grew up in New York and lived in London – until she returned in 1980 to Hong Kong.

INDEX AND GLOSSARY

YWCA ⇒